Linking Wilderness Research and Management

Volume 2—Defining, Managing, and Monitoring Wilderness Visitor Experiences:

An Annotated Reading List

Series Editor

Vita Wright
Research Application Program Director
Aldo Leopold Wilderness Research Institute
Rocky Mountain Research Station
U.S. Department of Agriculture, Forest Service
Missoula, MT 59801

Authors

Brian Glaspell
Social Science Research Assistant
Aldo Leopold Wilderness Research Institute
U.S. Department of Agriculture, Forest Service
Missoula, MT 59801

Annette Puttkammer
Research Associate
University of Montana Foundation
Missoula, MT 59807
(formerly with the Aldo Leopold
Wilderness Research Institute)

USDA Forest Service
General Technical Report RMRS-GTR-79-vol. 2.

September 2001

Preface

Federal land management agencies have recognized the importance of incorporating the best available scientific knowledge into management decisions. However, both managers and researchers have struggled to identify effective processes for accomplishing this objective. The Aldo Leopold Wilderness Research Institute's Research Application Program works toward understanding barriers to the use of science in management and toward developing ways to make relevant scientific information more accessible. Managers can base their decisions on the best available scientific knowledge only if they are aware of current and relevant science as well as how it fits into their management goals.

The Linking Wilderness Research and Management series of annotated reading lists was developed to help land managers and others access scientific information relevant to protecting and restoring wilderness and similarly managed lands, as well as the myriad of values associated with such lands. References in these reading lists have been categorized to draw attention to the relevance of each publication, and then organized to provide a logical framework for addressing the issue. Each volume begins with references necessary to understand the overall issue, and then provides references useful for identifying management goals, understanding influences on those goals, and finally, for selecting and implementing management approaches. For example, the Wilderness Visitor Experiences volume begins with sections on wilderness values and how to measure/describe wilderness visitor experiences, then includes sections on influences to experiences, visitor satisfaction, and management techniques, and finishes by addressing planning, planning frameworks, indicators and standards, and monitoring. Within each section, articles have been annotated to clarify their relevance to that section and to highlight their importance for wilderness management.

These reading lists were designed to serve a wide audience. First, each list introduces generalists to the breadth of factors that should be considered when addressing a management issue. These volumes also enable specialists to maintain familiarity with research relevant to their discipline but outside their area of expertise. For instance, the Invasive Plants volume may be useful to a botanist who specializes in protecting rare species but is not familiar with the invasive plant literature. For those generally familiar with the concepts, this series facilitates access to literature that can add depth to their conceptual knowledge. Rather than produce comprehensive bibliographies, which may be unwieldy for those with limited time, the authors included overviews, the most current examples of literature addressing pertinent concepts, and frequently cited classic publications. These lists can provide a starting point for readers interested in more detail on specific subjects to conduct their own literature reviews.

To facilitate access to these lists and enable us to update them, the lists are also available through the Aldo Leopold Wilderness Research Institute's Web site (http://www.wilderness.net/leopold). The Leopold Institute is a Federal interagency research institute that focuses on ecological and social science research needed to sustain wilderness ecosystems and wilderness values. I hope this series will help sustain wilderness, similarly managed lands, and associated values by enabling managers, policymakers, educators, user groups, and others to access the best available science on the topics covered.

—Vita Wright, *Series Editor*

Acknowledgments

We wish to thank Alan Watson, David Cole, Dan Williams, and Linda Merigliano for their review comments on this reading list. We appreciate Dave Ausband's and Alison Perkins' help with proofreading, and thank the interagency Aldo Leopold Wilderness Research Institute, the USDA Forest Service, Rocky Mountain Research Station's Identification and Valuation of Wildland Resource Benefits Unit, and the interagency Arthur Carhart National Wilderness Training Center for their sponsorship of this project.

Contents

INTRODUCTION

The 1964 Wilderness Act calls for "…an enduring resource of wilderness…for the use and enjoyment of the American people" and lists among the attributes of wilderness "outstanding opportunities for solitude or a primitive and unconfined type of recreation." These statements confirm experiential opportunities as one of the primary purposes of wilderness. Furthermore, by signing the act into law, Congress declared that wilderness experiences are so important they are worthy of protection by national legislation. Wilderness experiences have been credited with everything from personal psychological benefits to formation of the national character. Heavy or growing use levels at many wilderness areas are proof that the public increasingly values the opportunity to experience wilderness firsthand.

In response to the fear that increasing use would threaten the experiential qualities of wilderness and wildlands, researchers with training in sociology, psychology, and anthropology began a focused program of outdoor recreation research in the 1960s. Although the initial focus was on determining objective visitor "carrying capacities" for protected areas, scientists soon found that the relationship between use numbers and wilderness visitor experiences is extremely complex. This research expanded to address the values that people hold for wilderness (including nonrecreation values), the types and dimensions of wilderness experiences, and factors that influence those experiences. Simultaneously, managers and scientists worked together to develop techniques and long-term planning frameworks to ensure that quality wilderness experiences continue to be available.

Whereas early wilderness stewards had few resources other than instinct and personal experience to guide them, managers today have access to a significant body of literature related to defining, managing, and monitoring wilderness experiences. In fact, the volume of available information can be confusing or even overwhelming. This reading list gathers together and organizes a representative sample of this information in a way that we hope will be useful to both managers and researchers.

SCOPE

This reading list provides an overview of the literature related to defining, managing, and monitoring wilderness visitor experiences. The list should be helpful to managers or researchers new to the topic, and also those seeking knowledge about specific aspects of wilderness experiences and management. Rather than developing an exhaustive bibliography of all of information available on this topic, we chose to focus on the scientific literature that we determined to be most useful for managers. We cited publications that provide an introduction to important topics, with the idea that those interested in pursuing a topic further will find the referenced works helpful for directing them toward additional resources.

The reading list emphasizes recent literature because Federal land management agencies require the "best available science" to meet legislative and policy mandates, and the best available science is often synthesized in recent papers. We attempted to include only works that were subject to some form of scientific review, and we generally omitted papers that were highly technical or jargon-filled in favor of others that seemed more accessible to a general audience.

Although not comprehensive, the sources cited here represent a significant portion of the topics addressed by the wilderness experience literature. Wilderness user conflict is one exception. Although conflict is a significant issue in wilderness use management and planning, the breadth and volume of information on conflict warrants more space than is available here. Readers interested in conflict can watch for a future volume devoted entirely to this topic.

ORGANIZATION

This reading list is divided into four major, numbered sections. For the reader with a limited wilderness background, the numbered sections represent a progression from broad values associated with wilderness to specific management and planning approaches. Readers with more experience might go directly to the section in which they are interested. Section I contains both philosophical and empirical papers that address values related to wilderness and wilderness experiences. Section II contains papers that describe wilderness experiences and specific dimensions of those experiences. Section III has references that describe various influences on wilderness experiences, and approaches to managing them. Section IV addresses long-term wilderness planning and monitoring.

Each major section is further divided into minor sections, and in some cases, subsections, within which the articles are alphabetized by author's last name. Each of these minor sections is prefaced by a paragraph introducing and summarizing the literature included within the section and highlighting key papers. Articles have been annotated to highlight their relevance to the section in which they occur, as well as their overall importance to wilderness management. To avoid duplication, annotations for papers relating to multiple topics are included in the section we judged most relevant. However such papers are cross-referenced in the other relevant sections as well.

ANNOTATED READING LIST

I. WILDERNESS VALUES

Wilderness management is both influenced by, and influential on, the range of values associated with wilderness. The authors in this section discuss the significance of wilderness values (McCloskey 1990; Myers and Close 1998; Williams 2000; Williams and others 1992a), measure their importance for various user and non-user groups (Haas and others 1986; Loomis and Walsh 1992; Manning and Valliere 1996; Parker and Koesler 1998; Trainor and Norgaard 1999), and consider value changes and forces of change amongst wilderness visitors and society in general (Roggenbuck 1990; Watson and Landres 1999; Watson and others 1996; Williams 2000).

Haas, Glenn E.; Hermann, Eric; Walsh, Richard. 1986. Wilderness values. Natural Areas Journal. 6(2): 37-43.

Annotation: This paper investigated the degree to which people value wilderness for reasons other than the recreational opportunities it provides. A sample of 529 wilderness visitors and nonvisitors, drawn from 1980 Colorado telephone directories, received a mailed questionnaire in which they were asked to rate the importance of 13 different wilderness values derived from the 1964 Wilderness Act. A total of two-hundred eighteen respondents ranked the 13 values of wilderness listed in the questionnaire as follows: (1) protecting water quality, (2) protecting wildlife habitat, (3) protecting air quality, (4) knowing that future generations will have wilderness areas, (5) knowing that in the future you have the option to go there if you choose, (6) providing recreation opportunities, (7) protecting rare and endangered species, (8) providing scenic beauty, (9) preserving unique plant and animal ecosystems, (10) conserving natural areas for educational and scientific study, (11) knowing wilderness areas exist, (12) providing spiritual inspiration, (13) providing income for tourist industry. The top three most important values were the same for both wilderness visitors and nonvisitors. The authors concluded that wilderness is valued for many reasons other than recreation, and that a singular focus on recreational values leads to underestimation of overall wilderness value.

Loomis, John; Walsh, Richard. 1992. Future economic values of wilderness. In: Payne, Claire; Bowker, J. M.; Reed, Patrick C., comps. The economic values of wilderness: proceedings of the conference; 1991 May 8-11; Jackson, WY.

Gen. Tech. Rep. SE-78. Asheville, NC: U.S. Department of Agriculture, Forest Service, Southeastern Forest Experiment Station: 81-90.

Annotation: Onsite recreation use of wilderness accounts for less than 50 percent of the total economic value of wilderness. This paper discusses three kinds of value that wilderness preservation holds for offsite or future visitors: option value, existence value, and bequest value. These three values are pure public goods; everyone can consume them without diminishing the resource. In addition, these values of wilderness are expected to increase over time as the supply of natural areas decreases.

Manning, Robert; Valliere, William A. 1996. Environmental values, environmental ethics, and wilderness management—an empirical study. International Journal of Wilderness. 2(2): 27-32.

Annotation: This study described in this paper was designed to explore the environmental values and ethics of wilderness visitors in Vermont. A mailed questionnaire asked respondents to rank 11 values of wilderness and also asked questions to assess their underlying environmental ethics and specific attitudes toward wilderness management actions. The top three most important wilderness values among respondents were: (1) aesthetic (wilderness as a place to enjoy the beauty of nature); (2) education (wilderness as a place to learn how things are connected ecologically); and (3) recreation (wilderness as a place to enjoy outdoor recreation activities). Respondents tended to subscribe to environmental ethics based on stewardship, utilitarian conservation, and radical environmentalism. Respondents who attached more importance to educational, therapeutic, and moral/ethical values of wilderness tended to have more purist attitudes toward wilderness management. (In this study, purism was defined as the degree to which respondents supported management actions in line with the spirit of the 1964 Wilderness Act). The authors concluded that the diversity of wilderness values held by visitors may make future wilderness management conflict inevitable. However, they also noted that, since many ethics and values are biocentric and dependent on maintaining ecological integrity, managers should give more attention to nonrecreation values and ecological protection.

McCloskey, Michael. 1990. Evolving perspectives on wilderness values: putting wilderness values in order. In: Reed, Patrick C., comp. Preparing to manage wilderness in the 21st century: proceedings of the conference. Gen. Tech. Rep. SE-66. Asheville, NC: U.S. Department of Agriculture, Forest Service, Southeastern Forest Experiment Station: 13–18.

Annotation: This paper addresses the basic questions: Why do people want wilderness? And, what are they seeking to find there? The author describes a taxonomy of wilderness values along a continuum from concrete to abstract. A use is described as the most concrete kind of value; it is a way that individuals or groups utilize wilderness to gain satisfactions. A benefit is slightly more abstract; it is described as an advantage enjoyed by society collectively. A value is the most abstract concept; it is a reason, rooted in philosophy and culture, for wanting wilderness. Values, or reasons for wanting wilderness, are grouped into two broad categories: biocentric and anthropocentric. Benefits are described as tangible or intangible. Uses are the most well-developed classification. Categories of uses include: introspective experiences, science and research, wildlife habitat, education and outdoor learning, personal development, enjoyment, subsistence, and economic.

Myers, Connie G.; Close, Liz. 1998. Wilderness values and ethics. In: Kulhavy, David L.; Legg, Michael H., eds. Wilderness and natural areas in eastern North America: research, management and planning. Nacogdoches, TX: Stephen F. Austin State University, Arthur Temple College of Forestry, Center for Applied Studies: 291–295.

Annotation: Understanding the range of wilderness values is critical for effective wilderness management. This paper was developed by staff at the Arthur Carhart National Wilderness Training Center to help managers understand the values underlying wilderness legislation, modern support for wilderness preservation, and wilderness management decisions. The authors' discussion of values is broken down by value type: personal and organizational. A series of questions relating to various wilderness management issues is presented for managers to evaluate their personal values. Organizational values present in the mission statements of the various wilderness management agencies and in public laws such as the 1964 Wilderness Act are discussed. The authors describe a value triangle based on the resource, law and policy (organizational values), and the need to serve people (personal/social values). They suggest that wilderness managers try to locate their decisions within the triangle.

Parker, Julia Dawn; Koesler, Rena. 1998. Urban populations as an impact on wilderness: a study of values in the Los Angeles Basin. In: Kulhavy, David L.; Legg, Michael H., eds. Wilderness and natural areas in Eastern North America: research, management and planning. Nacogdoches, TX: Stephen F. Austin State University, Arthur Temple College of Forestry, Center for Applied Studies: 245–249.

Annotation: This research was designed to assess the wilderness values of urban residents in Los Angeles, CA. Analysis of preliminary data from a mail survey revealed a great deal of support for wilderness from an ethnically and economically diverse respondent population. Among other items, respondents strongly agreed that wilderness contributes to the quality of the United States and that some areas of the United States should be set aside to prevent development by people. Respondents strongly disagreed with the statement, "There is very little value in undeveloped land."

Roggenbuck, Joseph W. 1990. American wilderness: a resource of multiple and evolving values. Proceedings: 18th annual hardwood symposium of the Hardwood Research Council; 1990 May 6–9; Cashiers, NC. Memphis, TN: Hardwood Research Council: 77–85.

Annotation: Wilderness values as articulated by American philosophers, writers, poets, and statesman have evolved over time. This paper traces the evolution of those values against the backdrop of changing American culture. Early American wilderness values were based on the existence of a frontier. They included independent thought, freedom, primitivism, and simplicity. Later, transcendental philosophers emphasized inspiration and spiritualism, then others emphasized nationalism, utilitarian values, virile sport, humility, and mental health. The values evident in the 1964 Wilderness Act represent a political compromise and a snapshot in time. Values have continued to develop and evolve through passage of the act and into the present. The author suggests that in the future important wilderness values will include spiritual values, preservation of natural ecosystems, land stewardship, and connections with the world wilderness community.

Trainor, Sarah Fleisher; Norgaard, Richard B. 1999. Recreation fees in the context of wilderness values. Journal of Park and Recreation Administration. 17(3): 100–115.

Annotation: This study investigated the relationship between statements of willingness to pay fees for wilderness use and descriptions of spiritual and intrinsic wilderness values. Data were collected via standardized, semistructured interviews with 100 day or overnight Desolation Wilderness users in July 1997. Sixty-nine percent of respondents acknowledged spiritual and intrinsic values of wilderness. Some visitors described going to wilderness as similar to going to church. They also described the intrinsic value of wilderness as a place not controlled or built by people. While respondents generally supported wilderness use fees, they did not feel that their willingness to pay was an adequate expression of the values they held for wilderness. The results suggest that economic and noneconomic values of wilderness may be incommensurable.

Watson, Alan; Landres, Peter. 1999. Changing wilderness values. In: Cordell, H. Ken, principal investigator. Outdoor recreation in American life: a national assessment of demand and supply trends. Champaign, IL: Sagamore Publishing: 384–388.

Annotation: Current research suggests that wilderness values are constantly changing along with general social trends. The major values emphasized by the early wilderness advocates were: experiential values; mental and moral restoration values; and scientific values. Since passage of the 1964 Wilderness Act, changing culture, technological advances, environmental changes, and diversification of the national economy have altered attitudes toward wilderness. Specific influences on wilderness values since 1964 have included awareness of wilderness impacts caused by recreation, media coverage of the beneficial role of ecological processes, scientific understanding, and development of natural areas. The authors of this paper present a model for understanding the role of values and value changes in wilderness management. General social trends lead to specific values and beliefs that are ultimately realized in the form of wilderness legislation, policy, and management actions. The benefits derived from wilderness protection are values in their own right, and these influence general social trends to create a constantly changing circle of values.

Watson, Alan E.; Hendee, John C.; Zaglauer, Hans P. 1996. Human values and codes of behavior: changes in Oregon's Eagle Cap Wilderness visitors and their attitudes. Natural Areas Journal. 16(2): 89–93.

Annotation: This study compared characteristics of visitors to Oregon's Eagle Cap Wilderness in 1965 and 1993. Some visitor characteristics changed in ways that suggest the values visitors held for wilderness had also changed. Specifically, visitors in 1993 were better educated, more likely to belong to conservation or outdoor organizations, and more supportive of efforts to protect the wilderness character of the area. In addition, they were more restrictive in the behaviors they considered appropriate in wilderness. Among other items, visitors in 1993 were more supportive of letting fires and insect outbreaks run their course and more likely to disagree that campfires and burying trash were acceptable behaviors. These responses are evidence of a deep commitment to the wilderness resource and a purist attitude toward wilderness behaviors. The authors suggest that social change in the region including in-migration, national focus on the region's natural resources, and a growing urban population, as well as educational efforts contributed to the changes between 1965 and 1993.

Williams, Daniel R. 2000. Personal and social meanings of wilderness: constructing and contesting places in a global village. In: Watson, Alan E.; Aplet, Greg H.; Hendee, John C., comps. 2000. Personal, societal, and ecological values of wilderness: sixth world wilderness congress proceedings on research, management, and allocation, volume II; 1998 October 24–29; Bangalore, India. Proc. RMRS-P-14. Ogden, UT: U.S. Department of Agriculture, Forest Service, Rocky Mountain Research Station: 77–82.

Annotation: This paper examines the process of socially constructing meanings and values for wilderness. Social construction refers to social, cultural, and political processes by which groups of people create shared meanings and understandings of a place. The notion that wilderness meanings and values are socially produced suggests that they are anchored in history and culture, rather than objective, visible properties of nature. Meanings and values for wilderness are cultural expressions used to define who we are. Wilderness values are linked to personal, cultural, national, and even biological identities. The author argues that globalization and modernization are problematic for wilderness because they destabilize meanings and values. Globalization brings different cultures and their values into contact, and modernization makes rapid change possible. Values are increasingly subject to contest and power relations. Therefore, it is important to examine not only the values that people hold, but where the values come from, how they vary from place to place, how they are negotiated in society, how they are used in conflict situations, and how they influence policy decisions. The author reminds environmental scientists, managers, and planners that their work is itself an effort that seeks, creates, contests, and negotiates the meaning of nature and wilderness.

Williams, Daniel R.; Patterson, Michael E.; Roggenbuck, Joseph W.; Watson, Alan E. 1992a. Beyond the commodity metaphor: examining emotional and symbolic attachment to place. Leisure Sciences. 14: 29–46.

Annotation: This paper addresses the importance of understanding emotional and symbolic values and ties to settings in relation to managing user conflicts and public involvement in planning. The authors describe the dominant approach to managing wilderness and other recreation settings in terms of a commodity metaphor—an engineering-like emphasis on manipulation of tangible natural resource properties to meet the needs of recreational users. This approach treats wilderness settings as means rather than ends and fails to capture the emotional and symbolic values that visitors often hold for wilderness places. A study was conducted to evaluate the degrees of place attachment (ties to a specific geographical location) and wilderness attachment (ties to places identified as wilderness or to the concept of wilderness itself) among visitors at three wilderness areas in the Southeastern United States and one wilderness in Montana. Results indicated that many visitors did indeed have strong feelings of place and/or wilderness attachment. The authors argue that place attachment is an important concept for managers and planners. The place perspective reminds them that visitors associate a range of intangible values with specific wilderness places, which helps explain why people often care so passionately about the management of a particular resource.

II. MEASURING AND DESCRIBING WILDERNESS EXPERIENCES

A. The Nature of Wilderness Recreation Experiences

A major goal of wilderness experience research has been to describe the dimensions and dynamics that make wilderness experiences unique. The authors in this section employ a variety of different methods in their attempts to better understand visitor experiences. Borrie and Roggenbuck (1996) and Scherl (1990) asked visitors to record elements of their experiences as they happened. Patterson and others (1998) conducted interviews with visitors immediately following their experiences, and Dawson and others (1998a) conducted interviews with wilderness user focus groups. Shafer and Hammitt (1995) used mail-back questionnaires to test their conceptual model of visitor experiences. Each of these approaches to investigating wilderness experiences provides useful insights for managers.

Borrie, William T.; Birzell, Robert M. 2001. Approaches to measuring quality of the wilderness experience. In: Freimund, Wayne A.; Cole, David N., comps. 2001. Visitor use density experience: proceedings; 2000 June 1–3; Missoula, MT: Proc. RMRS-P-20. Ogden, UT: U.S. Department of Agriculture, Forest Service, Rocky Mountain Research Station: 29–38.

Annotation: This is a synthesis paper that summarizes the various methods used to describe and measure the nature and quality of wilderness visitor experiences. The authors identify four general approaches to measuring recreation experiences including satisfaction-based, benefits-based, experience-based, and meaning-based approaches. Satisfaction- and benefits-based approaches have traditionally dominated in the research literature. However, the authors argue that while these approaches are useful for evaluating management performance, they offer little insight into the nature of the wilderness experience itself. Experience-based approaches, on the other hand, focus on individual psychological processes during recreation participation. Meaning-based approaches attempt to understand the nature of wilderness experiences within the broad context of participants' lives. The authors conclude that meanings-based approaches are particularly well suited to capturing the unique elements of wilderness experiences, but they emphasize that meanings-based research cannot provide prescriptive directions for managers.

Borrie, William T.; Roggenbuck, Joseph W. 1996. Describing the wilderness experience at Juniper Prairie Wilderness using experience sampling methods. In: Kulhavy, David L.; Legg, Michael H., eds. Wilderness and natural areas in Eastern North America: research, management and planning. Nacogdoches, TX: Stephen F. Austin State University, Arthur Temple College of Forestry, Center for Applied Studies: 165–172.

Annotation: This paper describes the use of a unique research method—the Experience Sampling Method (ESM)—to investigate wilderness visitor experiences as they happened in the Juniper Prairie Wilderness in Florida. The ESM involves asking visitors to carry electronic beepers that signal preprogrammed random points of time at which subjects fill out brief questionnaires. A total of 137 individuals completed 280 questionnaires during the study period in July 1994. Questionnaires were designed to reveal respondents' focus of attention, activity participation, and general preferences, and how these items changed over the course of respondents' trips. This approach allowed visitors to rate elements of their experiences as they happened, rather than asking them for a single judgment of the entire trip in a post-hoc questionnaire. Results revealed differences between visitors' experiences and evaluations of conditions during high- and low-use periods. The authors conclude that the ESM is a useful tool for understanding visitor experiences and eventually developing indicators of wilderness conditions. However, they express some concern over the use of electronic beepers in wilderness.

Dawson, Chad P.; Newman, Peter; Watson, Alan. 1998a. Cognitive dimensions of recreational user experiences in wilderness: an exploratory study in Adirondack Wilderness areas. In: Vogelson, Hans G., comp./ed. Proceedings of the 1997 Northeastern recreation research symposium; 1997 April 6–9; Bolton Landing, NY. Gen. Tech. Rep. NE-241. Radnor, PA: U.S. Department of Agriculture, Forest Service, Northeastern Forest Experiment Station: 257–260.

Annotation: Solitude or privacy have often been treated as the most important dimensions of wilderness experiences. The most common indicators used to measure solitude have been based on number of users or user encounters in a given wilderness. This approach has been attractive to managers because it suggests straightforward measurement (just count the number of users) and straightforward management techniques (regulate user numbers to limit encounters). However, there is increasing evidence that solitude is only one of many important dimensions of the wilderness experience. This paper describes an exploratory study to identify the multiple dimensions of wilderness visitor experiences. Four focus group interviews were conducted with wilderness user groups in the Adirondack area. A list of positive and potentially negative experience dimensions was compiled from the interviews. Positive dimensions included solitude, but also psychological, social, spiritual, exploration, inspirational, physiological, skills, and natural environment dimensions. Potentially negative dimensions included user and management impacts and user encounters.

Patterson, Michael E.; Watson, Alan E.; Williams, Daniel R.; Roggenbuck, Joseph R. 1998. An hermeneutic approach to studying the nature of wilderness experiences. Journal of Leisure Research. 30(4): 423–452.

Annotation: This paper is an example of the meanings-based approach to studying wilderness experiences. The authors describe their philosophical research framework as an "hermeneutic approach" that begins with the premise that wilderness recreation is an emergent experience motivated by the broad goal of acquiring stories that enrich one's life (this differs from the traditional research approach that assumes wilderness visitors are motivated to achieve specific, well-defined goals). Also, it assumes that "the nature of human experience is best characterized by situated freedom in which the environment sets boundaries that constrain the nature of the experience, but within those boundaries recreationists are free to experience the world in unique and variable ways." This research differed from many other studies because, rather than testing a model of experience or measuring predetermined wilderness experience dimensions, it asked visitors to describe their experiences in open-ended interviews. A total of 30 posttrip interviews were conducted with visitors to the Juniper Prairie Wilderness in Florida. Four coherent dimensions of the visitors' experiences were identified: challenge, closeness to nature, decisions not faced in everyday life, and stories of nature. The authors found that some visitors' experiences fit traditional goal-oriented models but others clearly did not. Also, they found that time spent reflecting on the just-completed trip was an important phase of the experience for many study participants. Thus, conditions at the nonwilderness canoe landing where Juniper Prairie visitors completed their trips had a greater impact on the nature and quality of their experiences than use levels inside the wilderness.

Scherl, Lea M. 1990. The wilderness experience: a psychological evaluation of its components and dynamics. In: Easley, A. T.; Passineau, Joseph F.; Driver, B. L., comps. The use of wilderness for personal growth, therapy, and education. Gen. Tech. Rep. RM-193. Fort Collins, CO: U.S. Department of Agriculture, Forest Service, Rocky Mountain Forest and Range Experiment Station: 11–22.

Annotation: This paper presents a proposed taxonomy of wilderness experience dimensions based on research conducted in the context of an Australian Outward Bound program. Data were collected from logbooks in which program participants recorded their impressions and feelings over the course of their wilderness trips. The contents of the logbooks were summarized and analyzed to develop a list of wilderness experience domains and domain attributes. The eight domains were identified as: emotional state, self, social setting, physical environment, physical state, effort, descriptive, and general thoughts. The two experience domains that dominated study participants' writings were self and social settings. Contents of the logbooks were also summarized for each day of the trip in order to describe the dynamic process of a wilderness experience. Self and social setting were dominant domains throughout the experience, and physical environment only became important as participants prepared for their solo days. The author points out that the wilderness program was effective at providing opportunities for self-evaluation, understanding, and reflection. However, group size and interaction hindered participants' awareness of the physical environment.

Shafer, C. Scott; Hammitt, William E. 1995. Congruency among experience dimensions, condition indicators, and coping behaviors in wilderness. Leisure Sciences. 17: 263–279.

Annotation: This paper explores the wilderness experience in terms of five descriptors provided in the 1964 Wilderness Act: natural, solitude, primitive, unconfined, and remote. The authors propose that these descriptors exist as broad experience dimensions, specific resource conditions, and behaviors that visitors use to cope with or control resource conditions. The authors propose a conceptual model in which the experiential dimensions are treated as goals that relate to visitor perceptions of wilderness conditions and lead to behaviors. The basic question addressed in this study is, to what extent do the five wilderness descriptors, in the form of visitor's experiential goals, extend to perceptions of conditions and ultimately to coping behaviors? For instance, to what extent does a visitor's focus on solitude influence that visitor's perceptions and behaviors? The authors conducted a survey of visitors to the Cohutta and Okefenokee Wilderness areas in the Southeastern United States to test their hypotheses. They found general support for their conceptual model. Surveyed wilderness visitors did appear to seek experiences that incorporate the conditions described in the Wilderness Act. In addition, they held different levels of importance for conditions based on their experiential goals, and they used coping behaviors to manage their own experiences in wilderness.

B. Solitude and Privacy

The 1964 Wilderness Act describes wilderness as a setting with "…outstanding opportunities for solitude or a primitive and unconfined type of recreation." For this reason, solitude has often been identified as an important dimension of wilderness experiences. The authors in this section explore opportunities for solitude in various settings (Stewart and Cole 1997; Watson 1995) and describe the nature of solitude (Hammitt 1994; Hollenhorst and others 1994) and the related concept of privacy (Dawson and Hammitt 1996; Hammitt and Madden 1989).

Dawson, Chad P.; Hammitt, William E. 1996. Dimensions of wilderness privacy for Adirondack Forest Preserve hikers. International Journal of Wilderness. 2(1): 37–41.

Annotation: Attempts to measure wilderness solitude have often been based on the number and distribution of users in a given wilderness area. However, past research has not shown a strong statistical relationship between wilderness user numbers and user experiences. While solitude is often defined as being alone or apart from usual associates, privacy is a multidimensional concept that implies a state of mind as well as a state of being. This paper describes a field test of a previously developed psychological scale to measure dimensions of privacy in wilderness. Mail surveys were sent to 298 Adirondack Forest Preserve hikers in 1994. Respondents were asked to rate the importance of 16 items on the Dimensions of Wilderness Privacy Scale. A factor analysis of the 16 items produced four factors: natural environment, cognitive freedom, intimacy, and individualism. The authors discuss each of the privacy scale factors, and conclude that their results were similar to those from other studies that applied the Dimensions of Wilderness Privacy Scale in different wilderness settings. The utility of the privacy scale for wilderness planning and management is briefly discussed.

Hammitt, William. 1994. The psychology and functions of wilderness solitude. In: Hendee, John C.; Martin, Vance G., eds. International wilderness allocation, management, and research. Fort Collins, CO: International Wilderness Leadership (WILD) Foundation: 227–233.

Annotation: This paper describes the development and testing of psychological scales designed to measure dimensions of wilderness privacy. The authors build on the theoretical work of others to define the related concepts of wilderness solitude and wilderness privacy. Privacy is described as a physical and psychological state of being that contains solitude as one of its dimensions. The other dimensions of privacy include intimacy, anonymity, and reserve. These four psychological dimensions perform four functions: personal autonomy, emotion release, self-evaluation, and limited and protected communication. Based on this theoretical model, two scales (Dimensions of Privacy and Functions of Privacy) were developed to measure how privacy operates among wilderness users. Each scale consisted of a number of items that wilderness users were asked to rate on a seven-point importance scale. The Dimensions of Privacy Scale was administered to Appalachian Trail hikers in Great Smoky Mountains National Park. The Functions of Privacy Scale was field tested in the Ellicott Rock Wilderness, located primarily in South Carolina. The items in each scale were analyzed to determine the underlying psychological dimensions and functions of wilderness privacy. The analysis identified five psychological dimensions and five functions of wilderness privacy that were related to, but slightly different from those described in the theoretical model.

Hammit, William E.; Madden, Mark A. 1989. Cognitive dimensions of wilderness privacy: a field test and further explanation. Leisure Sciences. 11(4): 293–301.

Annotation: This paper describes a field test of the Dimensions of Privacy Scale conducted in Great Smoky Mountains National Park. Backpackers who visited shelters along the Appalachian Trail were contacted and later mailed a questionnaire that contained, among other variables, the 20-item Dimensions of Privacy Scale. Respondents were asked to rate the importance of each of the items on a seven-point scale. Results of the field test were compared to results from a 1981 laboratory test of the privacy scale. Both the 1981 laboratory and 1987 field tests produced similar results. Factor analysis of results from the field test identified five psychological dimensions of wilderness privacy: natural environment, individual cognitive freedom, social cognitive freedom, intimacy, and individualism. Each of the dimensions is discussed in detail. The authors conclude that wilderness privacy provides a better and more useful concept of solitude than simply "being alone."

Hollenhorst, Steve; Frank, Ernest, III; Watson, Alan. 1994. The capacity to be alone: wilderness solitude and growth of the self. In: Hendee, John C.; Martin, Vance G., eds. International wilderness allocation, management, and research. Fort Collins, CO: International Wilderness Leadership (WILD) Foundation: 234–239.

Annotation: The authors of this paper explore the meaning of solitude as a beneficial component of the wilderness experience. They suggest that past research efforts have been limited by a frame of reference in which solitude is investigated in terms of its relevance to a community of others. For instance, much of the research motivated by questions about solitude has actually investigated privacy. According to the authors' review of past literature, privacy is essentially about control of transactions with others. In contrast, the authors propose that solitude is essentially about control of the self. The true determinant of solitude is the capacity to utilize time spent alone to achieve self-related benefits. Solitude is a state of mind as well as a state of being. The authors conducted a survey to test their conceptual hypothesis at five National Forest wilderness areas in the Eastern United States. The majority of respondents were visitors to the Dolly Sods Wilderness area in West Virginia. Based on initial analysis of the survey results, the authors present several points: solitude conceptually differs from privacy, aloneness is a necessary condition of solitude, there are hierarchical levels of solitude achievement, crowding perceptions and encounter numbers are weak predictors of solitude achievement, and the most effective predictors of solitude achievement are predispositional factors that visitors bring with them. The authors conclude that wilderness managers should address solitude not only by providing opportunities for aloneness, but also by educating, nurturing, and promoting the capacity for solitude in wilderness users.

Stewart, William P.; Cole, David N. 1997. Truths about solitude at Grand Canyon. In: Harmon, David, ed. Making protection work: proceedings of the 9th conference on research and resource management in parks and on public lands; 1997 March 17–21; Albuquerque, NM. Hancock, MI: George Wright Society: 21–24.

Annotation: The authors' stated purpose for this paper is to expose some myths associated with management of solitude and crowding in backcountry areas. In order to counter the identified myths, they present some general statements supported by empirical evidence from several studies conducted at Grand Canyon National Park. The authors begin by addressing the practice of dividing backcountry areas into zones based on level of development. A common assumption has been that undeveloped areas attract visitors seeking solitude while more developed zones are "sacrifice areas" where visitors have no hope or expectation of achieving solitude. However, a 1984 to 1985 Grand Canyon study revealed that all zones attract visitors seeking solitude. Another common practice in solitude research has been the use of one-time, mail-back questionnaires as measurement instruments. The authors explain how different situational and respondent attributes can confound the interpretation of results from these studies. Lastly, although research has alternately focused on managerial and nonmanagerial factors as the primary influences on solitude, the authors suggest that both types of factors have consistent influence. The authors conclude by stating that recognition of the diversity of environments that provide solitude is the first step in improving its management.

Watson, Alan E. 1995. Opportunities for solitude in the Boundary Waters Canoe Area Wilderness. Northern Journal of Applied Forestry. 12(1): 12–18.

Annotation: This paper presents the results of an applied study aimed at improving opportunities for solitude in the Boundary Waters Canoe Area Wilderness in Minnesota. The study was designed to examine the relationship between visitor reports of use densities, density preferences, density tolerances, and density expectations in reference to opportunities for solitude. Results from a 1991 survey mailed to 398 Boundary Waters visitors led to three suggested indicators for evaluating solitude opportunities: the proportion of visitors who have difficulty finding an unoccupied campsite, the number of user encounters deemed acceptable by visitors versus the actual number of encounters, and the proportion of visitors for whom the number of user encounters was unacceptable even on the lowest encounter day. The author concludes that, given existing use levels, a Forest Service proposal to restrict visitation could offer benefits to visitors. However, management objectives based on visitors' preference levels may change as visitors become more (or less) tolerant of encounters. The author suggests further examination of the potential problems caused by changing societal or individual definitions of solitude.

C. Spiritual Experience Dimensions

Spiritual experience in wilderness is often described as a feeling of oneness with nature. Spiritual experiences are a common theme in wilderness literature, but they are rarely incorporated into management goals or decisionmaking. The authors in this section discuss various uses of wilderness for spiritual purposes and describe setting features and trip characteristics that facilitate spiritual experiences.

Fredrickson, Laura M.; Anderson, Dorothy H. 1999. A qualitative exploration of the wilderness experience as a source of spiritual inspiration. Journal of Environmental Psychology. 19: 21–39.

Annotation: This paper describes characteristics of physical and social settings that were important influences on the spiritually inspirational qualities of two separate wilderness group trips. Data were collected from trip journals and indepth interviews with participants from all-women wilderness trips in the Boundary Waters Canoe Area Wilderness and the inner plateau of the Grand Canyon. Two dominant themes that emerged from the data were the importance of being in an all-women's group and the resulting social interaction, and the importance of being in a genuine or bona fide wilderness environment. Being in an all-women's group facilitated group trust and emotional safety, sharing of common life changes, and a noncompetitive atmosphere. Being in a wilderness environment facilitated direct contact with nature, periods of solitude, and physical challenge. In combination, these attributes contributed to an experience that most participants described as spiritually inspirational. Feelings that participants associated with spirituality included: empowered, hopeful, grounded and secure, wonder and awe, and humility. Participants in the Grand Canyon trip more frequently spoke about individual features of the environment in relation to their feelings than did participants who traveled in the Boundary Waters. The authors speculate that the lush vegetation and lack of topographical relief in the Boundary Waters led participants there to perceive the landscape as more of an "organistic whole." In contrast, the stark landscape and panoramic views in Grand Canyon influenced participants to focus on dominant, individual features of the physical environment. The authors conclude that the expansive landscape and unmodified, untamed nature of the wilderness areas visited were the fundamental aspects of the trips that provoked spiritual feelings.

McDonald, Barbara; Guldin, Richard; Wetherhill, Richard. 1989. The spirit in the wilderness: the use and opportunity of wilderness experience for spiritual growth. In: Freilich, Helen R., comp. Wilderness benchmark 1988: proceedings of the national wilderness colloquium; 1988 January 13–14; Tampa, FL. Gen. Tech. Rep. SE-51. Asheville, NC: U.S. Department of Agriculture, Forest Service, Southeastern Forest Experiment Station: 193–207.

Annotation: This paper discusses spiritual values and opportunities for spiritual experiences and growth in wilderness. The authors suggest that spiritual dimensions of wilderness value and wilderness experiences have been relatively unexplored by researchers because a concise operational definition of spiritual experience or growth has not been developed. In response to this problem, they offer this definition of spirituality: Wilderness spirituality refers generally to the development of an emotional or mental awareness of fundamental interrelationships among all naturally occurring things. When this awareness occurs suddenly it is spiritual experience. When it happens gradually over time it is called spiritual growth. As a general management guideline, the authors suggest that the more natural, unconfused, and peaceful a wilderness setting, the more likely it is that an individual may reflect on interrelationships and subsequently have a spiritual experience. Although spiritual opportunities exist in virtually any setting, the authors suggest that wilderness managers consider enhancing or maintaining spiritual opportunities by evaluating attributes such as proximity to wildlife, auditory protection from human-made sounds, outstanding aesthetic opportunities, open and expansive or closed-in and protective areas, high places, water resources, and environmental quality and integrity.

Riley, Marilyn Foster; Hendee, John C. 2000. Wilderness vision quest clients: motivations and reported benefits from an urban-based program 1988 to 1997. In: Watson, Alan E.; Aplet, Greg H.; Hendee, John C., comps. Personal, societal, and ecological values of wilderness: Sixth World Wilderness Congress proceedings on research, management, and allocation, volume II; 1998 October 24–29; Bangalore, India. Proc. RMRS-P-14. Ogden, UT: U.S. Department of Agriculture, Forest Service, Rocky Mountain Research Station: 128–135.

Annotation: This article describes a study of the experiences and benefits received by participants in a wilderness vision quest program. Wilderness vision quests are three-stage processes modeled after traditional rites of passage from indigenous cultures. They involve a preparation stage, completion of a fasting time alone in nature, and entry back into daily life. The authors estimate that there are about 50 active vision quest programs worldwide. Data for this study were collected by mailing a questionnaire to persons who were clients of a vision quest program, Wilderness Transitions, Inc., during the period 1988 through 1997. Results indicated that the most important reasons for going on vision quests were "spiritual journey" and "self discovery." Respondents also listed benefits they received as a result of their experiences. Based on an analysis of the survey data, the authors suggest a process by which self-discovery leads to spiritual experience. Survey respondents indicated that their experiences were strongly wilderness dependent, citing naturalness and solitude as essential conditions for personal benefits they received.

Stringer, L. Allison; McAvoy, Leo H. 1992. The need for something different: spirituality and wilderness adventure. Journal of Experiential Education. 15(1): 13–20.

Annotation: This paper describes a study to investigate spiritual development and the nature of spiritual experiences in the context of wilderness adventure programs. The subjects of the study were participants in two wilderness adventure programs in 1987. The first group consisted of 13 persons with and without physical disabilities on an 8-day canoe trip in Northern Ontario. The second group consisted of 18 wilderness leadership students (13 of whom participated in the study) on a 10-day backpacking trip in Wyoming and Montana. Data were collected from four sources: pretrip questionnaires, onsite observations, posttrip interviews, and analyses of trip journals. Although very few participants listed spiritual goals in their pretrip questionnaires, common themes related to spirituality emerged from both groups. These themes included: the shared spirit between people; a power greater than self; clarity of self-knowledge; inner feelings; awareness of the world and one's place in it; and others. Most participants noted that their opportunities to experience spirituality were greatly increased by being in the wilderness. The authors provide detailed lists of factors that contributed to or inhibited spiritual experiences. Increased opportunities for spiritual experiences were generally attributed to the absence of constraints that people usually have in their everyday lives. A list of conclusions and recommendations for enhancing spiritual experience opportunities is given.

Trainor, Sarah Fleisher; Norgaard, Richard B. 1999. Recreation fees in the context of wilderness values. Journal of Park and Recreation Administration. 17(3): 100–115.

Annotation: See section I, page 6.

D. Wilderness for Personal Growth, Therapy, and Education

Wilderness is increasingly being used as a tool for developmental, therapeutic, and educational purposes. The authors in this section investigate how wilderness facilitates these purposes (Easley and others 1990; Scherl 1989; White and Hendee 2000; Williams and others 1989) and describe the nature and function of Wilderness Experience Programs (WEPs), which are designed to provide visitors with developmental wilderness benefits (Dawson and others 1998b; Gager and others 1998; Russell and others 1998).

Dawson, Chad P.; Tangen-Foster, Jim; Friese, Gregory T.; Carpenter, Josh. 1998b. Defining characteristics of U.S.A. wilderness experience programs. International Journal of Wilderness. 4(3): 22–27.

Annotation: One of the most popular ways that people use wilderness for personal growth, therapy, and education is through participation in Wilderness Experience Programs. The purpose of this article is to classify Wilderness Experience Programs (WEPs) and characterize their program aims, methods, and time spent in wilderness. WEPs are defined by three criteria: they provide experiences and activities that are dependent on wilderness conditions; they provide experiences and activities that are consistent with wilderness use; and they include interpersonal and intrapersonal activities that enhance personal development. The single defining characteristic of WEPs is the central role of wilderness to program experience and delivery. A 1996 study by coauthor Friese proposed classifying WEPs by their primary aims—either personal growth, education, or therapy and healing. Building on that study, this paper describes a survey of 330 WEP organizations to test the classification system proposed by Friese and determine other WEP characteristics. Results from the survey generally supported Friese's classification system. In addition, 67 percent of WEPs reported that wilderness is necessary for delivery of their programs, although most WEPs spent 50 percent or less of their total time in wilderness areas. The authors conclude that managers' abilities to promote wilderness stewardship to WEPs may be dependent on the type of WEP. An additional important conclusion for managers is that some WEPs may be delivered successfully in areas with wilderness characteristics that are not Federally designated as wilderness.

Easley, A. T.; Passineau, Joseph F.; Driver, B. L., comps. 1990. The use of wilderness for personal growth, therapy, and education. Gen. Tech. Rep. RM-193. Fort Collins, CO: U.S. Department of Agriculture, Forest Service, Rocky Mountain Forest and Range Experiment Station. 197 p.

Annotation: This conference proceedings contains 32 articles pertaining to the use of wilderness for human development. Beginning with an introductory article on the benefits of wilderness, topics covered include: psychological components of wilderness experience, Outward Bound and NOLS wilderness experience programs, wilderness therapy, and wilderness education. Although most of the articles pertain directly to the use of wilderness for personal growth, therapy, or education, there are also a few articles related to peripheral subjects such as wilderness as a focus for culture and art.

Gager, Dan; Hendee, John C.; Kinziger, Mike; Krumpe, Ed. 1998. What managers are saying—and doing—about wilderness experience programs. Journal of Forestry. August: 33–37.

Annotation: Wilderness experience programs, designed to provide personal growth, therapy, education, or group development, are perceived to be a rapidly increasing form of wilderness use. This paper describes a nationwide survey of Federal wilderness managers designed to explore four topics: agency policies and regulations for managing wilderness experience programs; wilderness managers' attitudes toward and concerns about them, and managers' suggestions for addressing those concerns. Results from the survey indicate that managers want to see higher standards and more regulation of wilderness experience programs. In addition, most managers do not feel that wilderness experience programs are wilderness dependent. The authors suggest that wilderness experience program leaders need to recognize how managers feel about their programs and work to improve cooperation and communication with them.

Russell, Keith; Hendee, John C.; Cooke, Steve. 1998. Social and economic benefits of a U.S. wilderness experience program for youth-at-risk in the Federal Job Corps. International Journal of Wilderness. 4(3): 32–38.

Annotation: Based on the theory that wilderness experience can increase self-esteem and sense of personal control, this article describes the benefits of a wilderness experience program for individuals in the Federal Job Corps. Participants in the wilderness program reported positive feelings such as empowerment and clarity. They also demonstrated an average 23.2 percent reduction in termination rate from the Job Corps, when compared to controls. A cost-benefit analysis was used to determine the net social benefits of implementing a wilderness experience program as an adjunct to the Job Corps program. Results of the analysis showed that for every dollar invested in the wilderness program, $1.52 would be returned.

Scherl, Lea M. 1989. Self in wilderness: understanding the psychological benefits of individual-wilderness interaction through self-control. Leisure Sciences. 11: 123–135.

Annotation: This paper addresses the need to understand how wilderness settings and wilderness experiences can promote both personal change and psychological well being. Using the multidimensional concept of control, the author explores possible human-wilderness relationships and interactions. The opportunity to exert self-control is proposed as the primary psychologically rewarding component of wilderness experiences. The author suggests that the nonresponsiveness of the wilderness environment to individual behavior and the need to use self-control to mediate environmental transactions are important and unique elements of wilderness experiences. In combination, these factors provide significant opportunities for personal growth.

White, Dave D.; Hendee, John C. 2000. Primal hypotheses: the relationship between naturalness, solitude and the wilderness experience benefits of development of self (DOS), development of community (DOC) and spiritual development (SD). In: McCool, Stephen F.; Cole, David N.; Borrie, William T.; O'Loughlin, Jennifer, comps. Proceedings: wilderness science in a time of change conference—volume 3: wilderness as a place for scientific inquiry; 1999 May 23–27; Missoula, MT. Proc. RMRS-P-15-VOL-3. Ogden, UT: U.S. Department of Agriculture, Forest Service, Rocky Mountain Research Station: 223–227.

Annotation: This paper describes and tests the relationship between wilderness attributes of naturalness and solitude and three categories of human benefits—development of self (DOS), development of community (DOC), and spiritual development (SD). The authors describe the assertion that naturalness and solitude can generate each of these human benefits as the "primal hypotheses." The DOS category includes a variety of previously reported, self-related benefits of wilderness experience including personal growth, restored functioning, self-actualization, self-control, self-efficacy, reduced anxiety, and others. DOC refers to benefits accrued as group qualities such as cooperation, open communication, and problem-solving ability develop during wilderness experiences. SD refers to feelings of connection to the larger universe, a higher power, nature, or a general feeling of "oneness." In a study of 44 wilderness users in Montana, Idaho, and Oregon, the authors found positive relationships between naturalness and solitude and the benefit categories DOS, DOC, and SD. These results provide support for the notion that wilderness management should focus on maintaining naturalness, and that solitude attributes will produce benefits for visitors.

Williams, Daniel R.; Haggard, Lois M.; Schreyer, Richard. 1989. The role of wilderness in human development. In: Freilich, Helen R., comp. Wilderness benchmark 1988: proceedings of the National Wilderness Colloquium; 1988 January 13–14; Tampa, FL. Gen. Tech. Rep. SE-51. Asheville, NC: U.S. Department of Agriculture, Forest Service, Southeastern Forest Experiment Station: 169–180.

Annotation: The authors of this article discuss the idea that opportunities to express and affirm self-identity through wilderness can facilitate human growth and development. Wilderness can provide people with a sense of who they are through its use as a symbol. It acts as an object or environment that represents abstract human values, beliefs, and characteristics. The authors present and discuss three levels of self-definition or identity: personal self, cultural self, and biological self. Cultural and biological identities are benefits that accrue to a larger population than the community of wilderness recreation users. The authors conclude with suggestions for future research and a plea for incorporating the human development benefits of wilderness into management and policy decisions.

III. MANAGING WILDERNESS VISITOR EXPERIENCES

A. Influences on Visitor Experiences

Managers charged with providing opportunities for quality wilderness experiences may benefit from an improved understanding of the various factors that influence those experiences. While visitor use may impact both physical and social setting elements in wilderness, visitors and managers alike may perceive these impacts differently. The authors in the first two subsections below investigate perceptions of visitor-use impacts and describe methods for incorporating those perceptions into management policy and practices. The papers in the third subsection focus on an emerging threat to wilderness experiences—technology. The authors in this section identify technological trends, describe how technological advances might influence the nature and meaning of wilderness experiences, and offer suggestions for evaluating the appropriateness of technology in wilderness.

1. Biophysical Resource Impacts

Cole, David N. 1996. Wilderness recreation in the United States: trends in use, users, and impacts. International Journal of Wilderness. 2(3): 14–18.

Annotation: This article reviews the results of several studies designed to increase understanding of trends in wilderness recreation. Use data, campsite and trail conditions, and visitor characteristics during various periods between 1965 and 1994 were analyzed. The author estimates that wilderness recreation use increased sixfold between 1964 and 1994. Despite this increase, visitor evaluations of campsite conditions have been relatively stable over time. The overall condition of trail systems in the Bitterroot-Selway Wilderness in Montana did not change significantly between 1978 and 1989. However, campsite impacts at three wilderness areas in Montana and Oregon increased dramatically, primarily as a result of new campsite establishment. The author warns that continued increases in recreation use will likely lead to greater wilderness impacts and crowding problems. He calls for direct action by management, including implementing use limits, when unacceptable conditions are identified.

Cole, David N.; Watson, Alan E.; Hall, Troy; Spildie, David. 1997. High-use destinations in wilderness: social and biophysical impacts, visitor responses, and management options. Res. Pap. INT-RP-496. Ogden, UT: U.S. Department of Agriculture, Forest Service, Intermountain Research Station. 30 p.

Annotation: See section III.A.2, page 17.

Martin, Steven, R.; McCool, Stephen F.; Lucas, Robert C. 1989. Wilderness campsite impacts: do managers and visitors see them the same? Environmental Management. 13(5): 623–629.

Annotation: Ecological impacts caused by recreation use in wilderness tend to be limited to a small percentage of land area within most wilderness areas. However, they can cause serious localized damages that affect visual qualities and thus visitor experiences. This article describes a study designed to explore visitor and manager perceptions of the amount and acceptability of wilderness campsite impacts. The study used artistic representations of campsites with overlays depicting various levels of bare ground, tree damage, and fire-ring impacts. Wilderness visitors were more likely than managers to find the represented conditions unacceptable. Although visitors and managers differed in their evaluations of the level of impacts, they agreed on the relative acceptability of different types of impacts. Bare ground was least acceptable, followed by tree damage, and then fire rings. The results indicate that amount of bare ground may serve as a good indicator for monitoring wilderness campsite conditions.

Roggenbuck, J. W.; Williams, D. R.; Watson, A. E. 1993. Defining acceptable conditions in wilderness. Environmental Management. 17(2): 187–197.

Annotation: This article describes an effort to compare visitor perceptions of acceptable conditions across four different wilderness areas: Cohutta, GA; Caney Creek, AR; Upland Island, TX; and Rattlesnake, MT. A mail-back questionnaire was sent to study participants to determine how important each of 19 potential indicators of social and physical conditions were to defining the quality of their wilderness experience. There was generally high agreement in mean visitor ratings across the four wilderness areas, but visitor opinions within a given wilderness varied widely. Among the most important indicators of wilderness quality were the amount of litter and the number of damaged trees around a campsite. The authors discuss these results and explain why using visitor rankings is necessary but not sufficient for selecting management plan indicators and standards. For instance, although they were ranked 1st through 19th, there was no statistical difference in influence between some of the top indicators. In other words, the influence of the fifth most important indicator could not be distinguished from that of the eighth. The authors suggest selecting indicators that cover the range of variation in visitor ratings and are highly influential. For managers, the results of this study indicate that site impacts do indeed play an important role in visitor experiences, clearly more so than overall amount of wilderness use.

Shelby, Bo; Harris, Richard. 1985. Comparing methods for determining visitor evaluations of ecological impacts: site visits, photographs, and written descriptions. Journal of Leisure Research. 17(1): 57–67.

Annotation: This article describes and contrasts methods for capturing user evaluations of ecological impacts caused by recreation use in wilderness. The ideal method might be to have people actually visit and evaluate campsites with different degrees of impact. Because this approach is not practical in many cases, alternative methods are necessary. For this study, the authors compared visitor impact evaluations based on site visits with evaluations based on site photographs, and written site descriptions. Visitors to the Mt. Jefferson Wilderness in Oregon were randomly selected to evaluate the same sites using one of the three methods. Evaluations based on photographs agreed with those from site visits 90 percent of the time. Evaluations based on written descriptions agreed with onsite evaluations 80 percent of the time. Where there was disagreement, the authors generally found that site representations did not accurately represent what would be the field of view for a site visitor. In addition, the authors suggest that photos and written descriptions may actually be better than site visits when the goal is to focus evaluation on a specific condition (such as bare ground). For these reasons, the authors conclude that photographs and written descriptions have encouraging potential for the development of standards for acceptable impacts.

Shelby, Bo; Shindler, Bruce. 1992. Interest group standards for ecological impacts at wilderness campsites. Leisure Sciences. 14: 17–27.

Annotation: The task of setting management standards for resource impacts in wilderness can be difficult if different user groups all have different standards. This article explores the issue of whether different groups have different standards for resource conditions. Interest groups—defined as organized bodies representing the shared attitudes or interests of a group—were surveyed to evaluate their standards for wilderness resource impacts. Interest group members were selected from hunting associations, backcountry horse clubs, an environmental organization, Explorer Scouts, hiking clubs, and Forest Service resource managers. Group standards were obtained by computing each group's mean acceptability rating for various campsites. Overall, fewer differences between the groups were found than past reports would suggest. However, there were some notable differences between managers, the

environmental group, and activity-oriented users. Managers tended to be the least tolerant of impacts, especially bare ground, and activity-oriented users were the most tolerant. Visitors in general were highly tolerant of campsite impacts, although the authors suggest that factors such as screening from other parties or the presence of a scenic view may increase visitors' tolerance for site damage.

Shelby, Bo; Vaske, Jerry J.; Harris, Rick. 1988. User standards for ecological impacts at wilderness campsites. Journal of Leisure Research. 20(3): 245–256.

Annotation: Traditionally, standards for ecological impacts have been based on expert judgments by managers. These standards are not useful for understanding the influence of impacts on visitor experiences, because managers and visitors may see impacts differently. This paper describes a model for conceptualizing and investigating user evaluations of ecological impacts in wilderness, then applies the model to a study of user standards for bare ground and fire rings in the Mount Jefferson Wilderness in Oregon. The authors explain the use of impact acceptability curves, and define three characteristics of evaluative standards: range, intensity, and crystallization. Range refers to the scope of acceptable conditions, intensity refers to the strength of feelings about impacts, and crystallization is a measure of group agreement. Results from structured interviews conducted with Mt. Jefferson Wilderness visitors indicate that users are willing and able to evaluate acceptable impact conditions (respondents avoided the neutral response category). Also, standards appeared to be different for different locations, although there was considerable agreement about overall impact standards.

Watson, Alan E.; Cronn, Richard. 1994. How previous experience relates to visitors' perceptions of wilderness conditions. Trends. 31(3): 43–46.

Annotation: This paper describes studies undertaken in Minnesota and California to investigate how past experience in a wilderness area influences visitor evaluations of social and resource conditions in that wilderness. The authors hypothesize that visitors with little or no experience cannot compare current to past conditions and will likely give less negative evaluations. Visitors at the Boundary Waters Canoe Area Wilderness and the Desolation Wilderness were asked to evaluate social and resource conditions then divided into three categories of past experience for analysis of the results. The categories were: (1) those who were on their first visit to that wilderness or had made their first visit inside the last 2 years; (2) those who made their first visit more than 2 years but less than 10 years ago; and (3) those who made their first visit more than 10 years ago. Results indicated that day users whose first visit was more than 10 years ago reported significantly more resource impact problems than the other less experienced groups. However, there were no significant differences between the overnight user groups. Overnight users of all experience levels were more likely to report impact problems than day users. The authors conclude that these results have important implications for managers. General visitor surveys in areas with a high proportion of first-time users may indicate that users are content with conditions when in fact conditions are deteriorating. In contrast, surveys in areas with many repeat visitors may provide more meaningful information.

Watson, Alan E.; Niccolucci, Michael J. 1995. **Conflicting goals of wilderness management: natural conditions vs. natural experiences.** In: Chavez, Deborah J., tech. coord. Proceedings of the second symposium on social aspects and recreation research; 1994 February 23–25; San Diego, CA. PSW-GTR-156. Albany, CA: U.S. Department of Agriculture, Forest Service, Pacific Southwest Research Station: 11–15.

Annotation: See section III.C, page 22.

2. Density and Crowding

Cole, David N. 2001. **Use density and wilderness experiences: a historical review of relevant research.** In: Freimund, Wayne A.; Cole, David N., comps. 2001. Density use and wilderness experience: proceedings; 2000 June 1–3; Missoula, MT. Proceedings RMRS-P-20. Ogden, UT: U.S. Department of Agriculture, Forest Service, Rocky Mountain Research Station: 11–20.

Annotation: This paper provides an historical review and synthesis of research that explores the relationship between use density and wilderness visitor experiences. Beginning with the carrying capacity concept, the author describes numerous past attempts to define and apply carrying capacity for wilderness management. Several summary points from the carrying capacity literature are presented: First, carrying capacity is not an inherent value; it is an evaluative judgment; second, carrying capacity judgments must necessarily favor certain uses and types of users; and third, use limits decisions should be made in the context of a large system. After reviewing the theoretical literature, the author proceeds with a review of empirical studies that attempted to determine carrying capacities or link experience quality with use density. Most studies of this kind used survey techniques, were conducted after wilderness trips, and required visitors to generalize about their entire experiences. The author suggests that these commonalities have limited research progress. Next the author reviews past studies of visitor assessments of appropriate wilderness use levels and visitor responses to use limits. A common finding from these studies is that visitors support use limits if overuse occurs, but they generally do not feel that overuse has occurred. At the end of the paper research needs are provided.

Cole, David N.; Watson, Alan E.; Hall, Troy; Spildie, David. 1997. **High-use destinations in wilderness: social and biophysical impacts, visitor responses, and management options.** Res. Pap. INT-RP-496. Ogden, UT: U.S. Department of Agriculture, Forest Service, Intermountain Research Station. 30 p.

Annotation: This paper describes a study conducted at three high-use wildernesses—Alpine Lakes, Mt. Jefferson, and Three Sisters in Oregon and Washington. The study quantified both visitor encounter rates and resource impacts caused by recreation use. In addition, exit interviews were conducted with visitors to understand their opinions of wilderness conditions. In all three wildernesses, encounter rates were high and resource impacts were substantial. Most visitors reported that resource impacts detracted from their experience, and they were supportive of intensive site management to mitigate campsite impacts. Despite encountering more people than they would have preferred, most visitors were not bothered by high user densities. Only 10 to 23 percent supported reducing use levels. The authors suggest that visitor education and intensive site management are preferable to use limitation as methods for mitigating the social and physical impacts caused by high use levels.

Hammitt, William E.; Patterson, Michael E. 1991. **Coping behavior to avoid visitor encounters: its relationship to wildland privacy.** Journal of Leisure Research. 23(3): 225–237.

Annotation: This paper investigates coping strategies that wilderness visitors employ to achieve desired experiences. Coping behaviors are used to make an environment more suitable for an individual or a group. They may involve physical actions or psychological adjustments. In wilderness, coping strategies may be employed when people are dissatisfied with the number of other users they encounter. For this study, backcountry campers at Great Smoky Mountain National Park were surveyed using a mail-back questionnaire. The campers were asked, among other items, how important solitude was to their experience and how often they used each of 12 different coping behaviors. Results of the survey showed that the most common coping strategy was camping out of sight of other groups. In general, physical coping behaviors were used more often than social or psychological behaviors. The authors speculate that visitors use physical strategies to avoid encounters, but when encounters occur, they seem willing to accept and comply with established norms for behavior and social interaction.

Hammitt, William E.; Rutlin, William M. 1995. **Use encounter standards and curves for achieved privacy in wilderness.** Leisure Sciences. 17: 245–262.

Annotation: A tremendous amount of effort has been devoted to understanding the relationship between use levels and wilderness experiences. The purpose of this paper is to present an alternative approach to understanding the use level-experience relationship. Whereas many past studies focused on the effect of encounter rates on perceived crowding, this study focused on the relationship between encounters and privacy. The authors hypothesize that privacy may be more closely related to encounters than crowding. After a review of past work related to crowding, the authors give a thorough explanation of the privacy concept. Privacy is defined as a state or level of social interaction that individuals seek to maintain. It is not the opposite of crowding, but rather a zone of acceptability along a continuum with crowding at one end. Crowding is defined as the outcome when people cannot regulate their encounters to achieve privacy. The authors conducted a study of visitors at Ellicott Rock Wilderness in the Carolinas and Georgia to explore the relationship between encounter rates and privacy. Responses to a mail questionnaire were used to construct privacy-encounter curves—visitor reported levels of desired privacy achieved, plotted against numbers of encounters. The curves indicated that privacy increased as encounters decreased until a certain point, after which encounters had little influence. The authors conclude that privacy served as a better dependent variable for investigating the encounter-experience relationship than crowding or satisfaction variables did in past studies. However, they caution that privacy is a complex concept that includes more than number of encounters. Also, the privacy-encounter relationship may not be meaningful for visitors with little desire or motivation for privacy.

Manning, Robert E. 1985. Crowding norms in backcountry settings: a review and synthesis. Journal of Leisure Research. 17(2): 75–89.

Annotation: This paper synthesizes the results of past studies that investigated the relationship between perceived crowding and backcountry recreation experiences. Many studies have treated crowding as a normative concept. That is, increasing use density is viewed as crowding only when it is perceived to interfere with a person's objectives or values. Thus, crowding studies have often sought to identify the specific factors that influence users' perceptions of crowding. The author of this paper reviews several of these factors in detail, including: motivations, preferences, and expectations of visitors; past experience of visitors; visitor attitudes; visitor demographics; type and size of groups encountered; behavior of those encountered; perceptions of alikeness; and situational variables such as type of area, location of encounters within an area, and environmental factors. Results of these studies indicate that there are a variety of crowding norms. Although selected groups appear to share common perceptions of crowding, there are different preferences and perceptions among the population as a whole. According to the author, these findings underscore the need for diversity in outdoor recreation opportunities. Also, the variety of factors that influence crowding perceptions offer managers opportunities to relieve crowding by adjusting use patterns and visitor behaviors, rather than setting use limits.

Patterson, Michael E.; Hammitt, William E. 1990. Backcountry encounter norms, actual reported encounters, and their relationship to wilderness solitude. Journal of Leisure Research. 22(3): 259–275.

Annotation: This paper describes a study to investigate congruency between stated encounter norms and reactions to actual conditions encountered in a backcountry setting. The authors describe normative theory as the idea that segments of society share standards or rules that prescribe what is acceptable in specific settings. A norm, therefore, is simply a shared standard. For this study, the authors identified norms for the acceptable number of encounters for backpackers seeking solitude in Great Smoky Mountains National Park, examined the backpackers reactions to encounters during an outing, and determined whether or not those reactions matched stated encounter norms. Based on results from a mailed questionnaire, the authors found that solitude was important to the experience of most backpackers. Most backpackers reported encounter levels that exceeded their norms both on the trail and at campsites. However, only 34 percent indicated that encounters detracted from their solitude experience. The authors provide a lengthy discussion and interpretation of these results. Among other things, they suggest that backpackers may not have salient encounter norms because solitude includes more than encounters; that their study may have measured beliefs rather than norms; and that the influence of encounters may be so dependent on factors such as behavior of those encountered that backpackers cannot predict the influence of encounters based only on encounter numbers.

Roggenbuck, Joseph W.; Williams, Daniel R.; Bange, Steven P.; Dean, Dennis J. 1991. River float trip encounter norms: questioning the use of the social norms concept. Journal of Leisure Research. 23(3): 133–153.

Annotation: Visitor perceptions and evaluations of crowding and other types of experiential and biophysical resource impacts are often assumed to be guided by social norms. As shared standards of acceptability, norms may provide planners and managers with a defensible basis for decisionmaking. Following a review and critique of past approaches to defining and measuring norms, this paper describes a study designed to expand and improve the utility of the social norms concept. A mail-back questionnaire was administered to whitewater rafters on the New River Gorge National River in West Virginia in order to assess the existence and consensus of norms for encountering other users on the river. A response rate of 67 percent yielded 616 useable questionnaires. Analysis of the questionnaires showed that a sizeable proportion of the rafters who indicated that encounters with others made a difference were unable to identify an acceptable number of encounters. In addition, there was generally low consensus among the norms that were reported, even for user subgroups that might have been more likely to have shared standards. The authors suggest that methodological differences and developments in the theoretical meaning of norms may account for the significant differences between their results and the results of past studies on recreation encounter norms. They also suggest that researchers and managers should proceed with caution when assuming the existence of social norms.

Shelby, Bo; Vaske, Jerry J.; Heberlein, Thomas A. 1989. Comparative analysis of crowding in multiple locations: results from fifteen years of research. Leisure Sciences. 11: 269–291.

Annotation: Most studies of crowding have focused on single populations or settings and individual-level analysis. This paper compares aggregate data from 35 studies to answer questions about how perceived crowding varies across settings, activities, research methods, and time. The authors found that perceived crowding has changed over time, and that resource availability, accessibility and convenience, and management strategies also influence crowding. Geographic region, participant activity, and research methodology did not appear to influence perceived crowding. The authors applied their results and experience to develop carrying capacity judgments and classify locations into one of five crowding categories. Locations where more than 80 percent of visitors feel crowded were judged to be operating over capacity. Locations where 65 to 80 percent of visitors feel crowded were judged likely to be operating over capacity. Locations where 35 to 65 percent of visitors feel crowded were judged normal, with those in the 35 to 50 percent range classified as low-normal and those in the 50 to 65 percent range classified high-normal. Locations where less than 35 percent of visitors feel crowded were unique and often had some management or natural factor that limited use.

Watson, Alan E.; Niccolucci, Michael J. 1995. Conflicting goals of wilderness management: natural conditions vs. natural experiences. In: Chavez, Deborah J., tech. coord. Proceedings of the second symposium on social aspects and recreation research; 1994 February 23–25; San Diego, CA.

PSW-GTR-156. Albany, CA: U.S. Department of Agriculture, Forest Service, Pacific Southwest Research Station: 11–15.

Annotation: See section III.C, page 22.

Williams, Daniel R.; Roggenbuck, Joseph W.; Patterson, Michael E.; Watson, Alan E. 1992b. The variability of user-based social impact standards for wilderness management. Forest Science. 38(4): 738–756.

Annotation: See section IV.C, page 27.

3. Technology

Borrie, William T. 2000. Impacts of technology on the meaning of wilderness. In: Watson, Alan E.; Aplet, Greg H.; Hendee, John C., comps. Personal, societal, and ecological values of wilderness: sixth world wilderness congress proceedings on research, management, and allocation, volume II; 1998 October 24–29; Bangalore, India. Proc. RMRS-P-14. Ogden, UT: U.S. Department of Agriculture, Forest Service, Rocky Mountain Research Station: 87–88.

Annotation: This short paper explores some of the possible impacts of technology on wilderness experiences and meanings. The author quotes from past works by a variety of philosophers. He warns that technologically mediated experiences and images of wilderness may alter what people expect from wilderness. Advances such as lightweight clothing and global positioning systems can make wilderness more comfortable and accessible, but there are costs in terms of the significance and value of wilderness. The author suggests that managers and policymakers carefully evaluate the benefits and costs of technology, and adopt a cautious policy to avoid unintentional incremental changes.

Freimund, Wayne; Borrie, Bill. 1997. Wilderness@internet: wilderness in the 21st century—are there technical solutions to our technical problems? International Journal of Wilderness. 3(4): 21–23.

Annotation: This paper attempts to organize the discussions about the role of information and communication technology in relation to wilderness. The authors question the adequacy of the 1964 Wilderness Act to provide guidance when dealing with technology issues in wilderness. For instance, should genetically enhanced or cloned packstock be allowed in wilderness? Two basic questions are offered as ways to evaluate the appropriateness of new technologies: (1) Who is benefiting from new technology? (2) How will the wilderness experience change as a result of new technology? The authors speculate on the ways that wilderness and experiences might change and suggest in conclusion that it is the concept of wilderness that is most vulnerable to foreseeable changes. Moreover, they suggest that the discussion about technology is one of values rather than of technical solutions.

International Journal of Wilderness. 2000. Special section: wilderness in the 21st century. 6(2): 9–26.

Annotation: This special section of the International Journal of Wilderness addresses issues of change and continuity for wilderness management in the next century. It is divided into three parts: visitors; activities and technology; and future roles. The second section contains four short articles from university faculty members and a wilderness program manager with the USDA Forest Service. These authors address potential impacts of technology on wilderness experiences and wilderness management practices. Author John Shultis recalls that automobiles were briefly opposed in National Parks but eventually won the day because they facilitated park use and public support for parks. He suggests that a similar debate is at hand concerning technology in wilderness. In the second article, Les Wadzinski hopes that wilderness laws will prevent change resulting from new recreation activities. In the third article, Doug Knapp calls for an approach to wilderness recreation that sheds technology at the trailhead. In the fourth article, Glenn Haas and Marcella Wells suggest that social and technological change will lead to a more pristine and highly prized wilderness system by 2050.

Strong, David. 1995. Crazy Mountains: learning from wilderness to weigh technology. Albany: State University of New York Press. 253 p.

Annotation: Rather than empirical research, this book contains a philosophical discussion of technology and the role of wilderness. The author critically examines the idea that technological devices and commodities make lives good. Using a planned development in the Crazy Mountains of Montana, the author discusses how wilderness can provide an alternative model for living to that offered by consumer culture. The first four chapters describe the wilderness setting and the looming conflict in the Crazy Mountains. In chapter 5, "The technological subversion of environmental ethics," the author explores the appeal of technology and the ways in which it can shape perception and experience. In the second half of the book, titled "Learning from wilderness," the author describes how nontechnological wilderness can provide an opportunity for people to learn to listen, consider, experience, speak, and ultimately to build, in better ways.

B. Visitor Satisfaction

Visitor satisfaction has long been a popular measure of the "quality" of wilderness experiences. However, research has revealed a number of limitations to the use of visitor satisfaction as a primary measure of wilderness experiences or as a guide for wilderness management. The papers in this section review the various applications of satisfaction concepts to outdoor recreation research and management, and identify factors that limit or complicate the use of satisfaction to guide management practices.

Manning, Robert E. 1999. Search for satisfaction. In: Studies in outdoor recreation: search and research for satisfaction (second edition). Corvallis: Oregon State University Press: 1–15.

Annotation: This book chapter serves as the introduction to a classic text on outdoor recreation research. The author begins the chapter by laying out the objectives for the book and tracing the development of outdoor recreation research. Next, he explains how visitor satisfaction has traditionally been used as a surrogate measure of quality by both managers and researchers. Satisfaction has most often been defined as the degree of congruence between expectations and perceived experiences. However, measures of overall satisfaction may be inadequate for several reasons: (1) satisfaction is a multidimensional concept and broad measures may not provide useful information about influential factors; (2) satisfaction is relative; (3) reliance on satisfaction as the measure of quality may lead to quality as defined by a low common denominator; (4) most studies have found uniformly high levels of satisfaction and may therefore have limited meaning for managers; and (5) satisfaction changes during and after experiences, and it is unclear what is the most appropriate time to measure it. The author concludes by emphasizing that, despite the limitations of overall satisfaction measures, satisfaction research has helped to reveal a variety of variables that influence recreational experiences.

Stewart, William P.; Hull, Bruce R., IV. 1992. Satisfaction of what? Post hoc versus real-time construct validity. Leisure Sciences. 14: 195–209.

Annotation: This article describes two different ways to conceptualize and measure recreation visitor satisfaction: post hoc satisfaction (PHS) and real-time satisfaction (RTS). PHS appraisal occurs sometime following a recreation experience. It is shaped by the combined influence of introspection, recall, and context. RTS is an appraisal of a recreationist's current state while engaged, onsite, in an activity. After a conceptual analysis that further differentiates between PHS and RTS, the authors discuss the appropriate uses of each measure. Next, they describe a research project conducted to investigate the relationship between PHS and RTS. Day hikers in the White River National Forest in Colorado were asked to rate their satisfaction with their experiences at various points during a hike and then immediately following the hike, and again 3 months and 9 months later. Statistical analysis of the results revealed that offsite evaluations were significantly different than those made during or immediately following the hike. Satisfaction at 9 months was unrelated to satisfaction during the hike. The authors conclude that PHS and RTS are distinct, and that the utility of either construct is dependent on the intent of the study. RTS may be more useful for evaluating the nature and quality of actual experiences, while PHS may be more useful for studies of long-term recreation benefits and future choice behavior.

Williams, Daniel R. 1988. Great expectations and the limits to satisfaction: a review of recreation and consumer satisfaction research. In: Watson, Alan, comp. Outdoor recreation benchmark 1988: proceedings of the national outdoor recreation forum. Gen. Tech. Rep. SE-52. Asheville, NC: U.S. Department of Agriculture, Forest Service, Southeastern Forest Experiment Station: 422–438.

Annotation: This article reviews and critiques the various ways that satisfaction has been approached in outdoor recreation research. The author's primary purpose is to examine the concept of satisfaction as a basis for evaluating recreation quality. The paper is divided into three main parts. The first section summarizes what outdoor recreation research has revealed about factors that influence satisfaction including crowding, goal attainment, and resource impacts. The second section covers conceptual issues underlying satisfaction measurement. In this section, the author reviews literature from the outdoor recreation and consumer behavior fields of study. In the final section, the author identifies limits to the use of

satisfaction for understanding outdoor recreation experiences and behaviors. Satisfaction treats recreation as a commodity among other consumer goods. However, since recreation is mostly self-produced, it is unclear what participants are evaluating when they respond to satisfaction questions—the resource, the managing agency, or their own performance. Satisfaction may not be an appropriate measure of quality, and it may not be a desirable goal of public policy. The author suggests that there is a larger context of quality that includes lifestyle, and it cannot necessarily be captured with a satisfaction measure.

C. Visitor Management Techniques

Techniques for managing visitor use may act directly on visitor behavior or rely on education and information to influence decisions that visitors make about appropriate behaviors. While some authors describe these different approaches as direct and indirect management techniques, others suggest that this classification is neither meaningful nor useful. For visitors, the relative subtlety or obtrusiveness of a management technique may be more important than whether it is classified as direct or indirect. In this section, the authors review the pros and cons of different management techniques (Lucas 1990; McCool and Christensen 1996; Watson and Niccolucci 1995), discuss specific techniques for addressing specific management problems (Cole 1989; Cole and others 1987; Doucette and Cole 1993), and describe the theory and application of persuasion and visitor education techniques for reducing impacts from visitor use.

Cole, David N. 1989. Low-impact recreational practices for wilderness and backcountry. Gen. Tech. Rep. INT-265. Ogden, UT: U.S. Department of Agriculture, Forest Service, Intermountain Research Station. 131 p.

Annotation: This report is intended to be used in combination with a second report entitled "Wilderness visitor education: information about alternative techniques." The annotation for both reports is given under Doucette and Cole (1993) below.

Cole, David N.; Petersen, Margaret E.; Lucas, Robert C. 1987. Managing wilderness recreation use: common problems and potential solutions. Gen. Tech. Rep. INT-230. Ogden, UT: U.S. Department of Agriculture, Forest Service, Intermountain Research Station. 60 p.

Annotation: This report is designed to be a troubleshooting guide for managers faced with specific wilderness recreation problems. The first section describes eight general strategies for dealing with problems: reduce use of entire wilderness, reduce use of problem areas, modify location of use, modify timing of use, modify type of use and visitor behavior, modify visitor expectations, increase resistance of the resource, and maintain or rehabilitate the resource. The authors differentiate among strategies, which are general approaches to mitigating problems, and tactics, which are specific approaches to implementing a strategy. Thirty-seven tactics are given and grouped according to common wilderness recreation problems. The bulk of the report describes each tactic in terms of its purpose, application, the extent of its current usage, estimated cost of implementation, likely effectiveness, and probable side effects. This report is organized as a sourcebook. Managers faced with a particular problem can go directly to a list of tactics for dealing with that problem, rather than reading the entire document from beginning to end.

Doucette, Joseph E.; Cole, David N. 1993. Wilderness visitor education: information about alternative techniques. Gen. Tech. Rep. INT-295. Ogden, UT: U.S. Department of Agriculture, Forest Service, Intermountain Research Station. 37 p.

Annotation: This report and Cole (1989) (see above) are designed to complement each. Together, they summarize information on low-impact wilderness recreational practices and management techniques for encouraging or enhancing these practices. Low-impact practices can reduce many common resource and visitor impact problems. The first report (Cole 1989) gives detailed descriptions of low-impact practices capable of mitigating common wilderness recreation problems. The author also provides a discussion and examples of messages designed to increase visitors' understanding of low-impact practices. The second report (Doucette and Cole 1993) provides a more indepth discussion of techniques for educating wilderness visitors about low-impact practices. The first portion of the report describes the results of a wilderness manager survey aimed at identifying existing educational programs in wilderness, their costs and effectiveness, and differences in programs between managing agencies. Two types of low-impact educational techniques were identified: media-based techniques that rely on brochures, maps, signs, interpretive displays, and the like; and personnel-based techniques that rely on direct visitor contact by agency employees. Results of the survey were compared to a similar study conducted 10 years previously, in 1980. Most educational techniques used in 1980 remained popular in 1990. However, use of personnel in the backcountry and in school programs increased during the decade. Managers did not consider any educational techniques they used to be highly effective, and they felt hindered by lack of funding for education. In the main section of the report, the authors describe a variety of educational techniques in detail, including some emerging and innovative new techniques. In the final section, some principles for effective wilderness education are given, and a list of references for further information is provided.

Lucas, Robert C. 1990. The wilderness experience and managing the factors that influence it. In: Hendee, John C.; Stankey, George H.; Lucas, Robert C. Wilderness management. Golden, CO: North American Press: 469–496.

Annotation: This book chapter begins with a summary of the factors that may influence wilderness experiences, then describes several indirect and direct management techniques aimed at protecting or enhancing those experiences. Indirect techniques are defined as those that influence visitors rather than directly controlling them. They include physical setting design, information and education, eligibility requirements, and fees. Setting design and visitor education are relatively common techniques, but eligibility requirements—such as a wilderness skills test—and fees have generally not been used to manage visitors. Direct management techniques restrict individual choices. They allow a high degree of control but may be costly for both managers and visitors. Examples of

direct management include party-size limits, length-of-stay limits, general-use rationing, and prohibition of certain types of use or practices (such as campfires). The authors provide examples and descriptions of actual use-rationing systems that have been applied in wilderness areas. Next, a brief discussion of experience quality monitoring is given, followed by a more lengthy description of use simulation models. Simulation models may allow managers to design plans without costly trial and error procedures. In the final section, the authors speculate on visitor management in the future, emphasizing the continued need for visitor education, and summarize the contents of the chapter.

McCool, Stephen F.; Christensen, Neal A. 1996. Alleviating congestion in parks and recreation areas through direct management of visitor behavior. In: Lime, David W., ed. Congestion and crowding in the National Park System: guidelines for management and research. Misc. Publ. 86-1996. St. Paul: University of Minnesota, Minnesota Agricultural Experiment Station: 67–83.

Annotation: The authors of this article give three objectives for their paper: first, to discuss conceptual issues associated with direct and indirect management; second, to summarize the results of past research on these techniques; and third, to suggest a research agenda to address identified knowledge gaps. Most literature advocates for indirect management techniques, especially in backcountry or wilderness settings where freedom and unconfined experiences are perceived to be highly valuable. However, some research has shown that managers feel direct controls are more effective than indirect techniques, and there may be other advantages to direct controls as well. For instance, regulations may preserve freedoms that visitors might not otherwise enjoy. The authors review research on the use of direct management techniques and present a summary of general research findings. Among other items they note that visitor support for direct management is lowest in wilderness settings, and highest in settings with a tradition of direct management. The authors present a two-dimensional model of management techniques, bounded by direct and indirect on the horizontal axis, and visible and subtle on the vertical axis. They suggest that direct and indirect techniques be viewed and applied in combination. The final portion of the article presents questions for future research to address.

Roggenbuck, Joseph W. 1992. The use of persuasion to reduce resource impacts and visitor conflicts. In: Manfredo, Michael J., ed. Influencing human behavior: theory and applications in recreation, tourism, and natural resources management. Champaign, IL: Sagamore Publishing.

Annotation: This book chapter discusses the use of persuasive communication as a management tool to reduce resource impacts, visitor conflicts, and vandalism or depreciative behavior in recreation settings. Beginning with a review of the nature and causes of resource and visitor impacts, the author then moves on to a discussion of the likely effectiveness of persuasion for reducing certain types of impacts. He suggests that effectiveness is dependent on type of impact, the behavior involved, and motives for the behavior. Next, the author discusses three conceptual routes to persuasion: applied behavior analysis, the central route to persuasion, and the peripheral route to persuasion. Applied behavioral analysis seeks to increase or decrease certain behaviors through prompts, manipulation of the environment, and rewards or punishments. The central route to persuasion is most common. The premise behind this approach is that recipients pay careful attention to persuasive message content and integrate message content into their existing belief systems. Managers know their audience and tailor their messages specifically for them. The peripheral route to persuasion is characterized by low attention by the recipient to the message content. Peripheral messages may influence behavior based on the authority or attractiveness of their source, rather than their content, and they are appropriate for busy or distracting environments. Following this section, the author uses reported findings from numerous past studies to systematically evaluate the effectiveness of persuasive approaches for causing certain types of behavioral change. A numbered list of general findings is given for each of the following categories: knowledge-attitude-behavior intention change; selection of different recreation places; and reducing resource impacts.

Vander Stoep, Gail A.; Roggenbuck, Joseph W. 1996. Is your park being "loved to death?": using communications and other indirect techniques to battle the park "love bug." In: Lime, David W., ed. Congestion and crowding in the National Park System: guidelines for management and research. Misc. Publ. 86-1996. St. Paul: University of Minnesota, Minnesota Agricultural Experiment Station: 85–132.

Annotation: This article begins with a discussion of the promise and limits of social science for solving visitor and resource management problems. The bulk of the paper is then focused on understanding the use of communications (indirect management) to reduce depreciative behavior, distribute use, reduce conflicts, and encourage resource protective behavior. The authors note that there has been a major movement toward use of communication as a management tool, and suggest two major questions resulting from this movement: (1) How can communication strategies be shown to be truly effective at addressing management problems? (2) How can these strategies be most effectively implemented and integrated with other management strategies? Next, a detailed review of conceptual approaches to understanding behaviors is given, followed by a detailed review of research literature related to indirect management techniques. At the end of the paper, following the References Cited section, a list of additional relevant readings is provided.

Watson, Alan E.; Niccolucci, Michael J. 1995. Conflicting goals of wilderness management: natural conditions vs. natural experiences. In: Chavez, Deborah J., tech. coord. Proceedings of the second symposium on social aspects and recreation research; 1994 February 23–25; San Diego, CA. PSW-GTR-156 Albany, CA: U.S. Department of Agriculture, Forest Service, Pacific Southwest Research Station: 11–15.

Annotation: This article describes a study designed to measure beliefs and attitudes underlying visitors' support for wilderness use restrictions. The study was conducted at the Three Sisters, Mt. Washington, and Mt. Jefferson wildernesses in Oregon. A mail survey was used to assess users' reactions to a new permit requirement and their attitudes toward potential use limits. A statistical technique was used to classify respondents into two categories: those who believed overuse had occurred and those who believed use limits were unacceptable. Sixty-three percent of day users and 44 percent of overnight users did not consider the permit requirement to be inconvenient. A large majority of visitors indicated that they supported use limits to protect wilderness qualities. However, only 20 percent of overnight users and 11 percent of day users felt use restrictions should be initiated immediately, indicating that most visitors believed overuse had not yet occurred. The best predictors of campers' attitudes toward use limits were a combination of crowded feelings and perceptions of trail and campsite impacts. Physical impacts were the most important factor for overnight users, while day users were more influenced by numbers of people.

IV. WILDERNESS MANAGEMENT PLANNING

A. Overview

The need to balance visitor experience opportunities and biophysical resource protection is a fundamental challenge faced by wilderness stewards. The basic purpose of wilderness management planning is to develop guidelines for addressing this challenge. The two articles in this overview section introduce the tenants of wilderness planning and review the various ways that planning has been approached.

Hendee, John C.; von Koch, Russell. 1990. Wilderness management planning. In: Hendee, John C.; Stankey, George H.; Lucas, Robert C. Wilderness management. Golden, CO: North American Press: 195–212.

Annotation: This book chapter is from a widely used text on wilderness management. It begins with an explanation of the need for planning and the requirements of the National Environmental Policy Act (NEPA), then describes basic processes for planning within each of the Federal wilderness management agencies. The bulk of the chapter describes a framework for preparing, writing, and evaluating wilderness management plans. The authors emphasize that planning is a decisionmaking process that seeks to attain clearly stated management goals and objectives. Example sections of plans from the Lee Metcalf, Alpine Lakes, and Frank Church-River of No Return Wilderness areas are provided. The authors also discuss public involvement and plan review processes, and present a list of 10 criteria for evaluating plans.

Manning, Robert E.; Lime, David W. 2000. Defining and managing the quality of wilderness recreation experiences. In: McCool, Stephen F.; Cole, David N.; Borrie, William T.; O'Loughlin, Jennifer, comps. 2000. Proceedings: wilderness science in a time of change conference—volume 4: wilderness visitors, experiences, and visitor management; 1999 May 23–27; Missoula, MT. Proc. RMRS-P-15-VOL-4. Ogden, UT: U.S. Department of Agriculture, Forest Service, Rocky Mountain Research Station: 13–52.

Annotation: This substantial paper uses the frameworks of carrying capacity and the Recreation Opportunity Spectrum (ROS) to organize and synthesize the sizeable body of literature on managing wilderness and wilderness experiences. The carrying capacity concept is at the heart of most popular planning frameworks including Limits of Acceptable Change, Visitor Impact Management, and Visitor Experience and Resource Protection. ROS is the basic conceptual framework for encouraging diversity in outdoor recreation opportunities. A fundamental feature of popular planning frameworks is the need for selection of indicators and standards of quality. The authors describe the basic theory behind indicators and standards, then provide lists of criteria for choosing them. In addition, they provide an analysis of theoretical and methodological issues related to normative standards for wilderness and outdoor recreation. The next section focuses on wilderness management practices. The authors provide a detailed review of theories and empirical studies related to the use of information and education for visitor management, and use rationing and allocation. The final section of the paper identifies the current status and trends in wilderness management, and suggests directions for future wilderness research and management.

B. Planning Frameworks

The planning frameworks described in this section are related in that they specify step-by-step methods for identifying area concerns and establishing limits or standards for significant impacts or indicators of change. The four frameworks are presented in approximate chronological order of development. However, the frameworks have evolved and continue to evolve as they are adapted for new applications. The Limits of Acceptable change framework has been widely used for planning in Forest Service and Bureau of Land Management wilderness areas, while the Visitor Experience and Resource Protection framework was developed specifically for National Park Service lands.

1. Carrying Capacity

Schreyer, Richard, guest ed. 1984. Theme issue: social carrying capacity. Leisure Sciences. 6(4): 387–507.

Annotation: This special journal issue contains seven articles focused on the issue of social carrying capacity in outdoor recreation settings. Although nearly 20 years old, these articles are important because they synthesize findings from the first 20 years of vigorous carrying capacity research and highlight issues that continue to trouble researchers and managers today. The first two articles provide an overview of the carrying capacity idea and briefly review ideas and themes developed since 1964, when carrying capacity was widely introduced to the outdoor recreation research community in a popular monograph. The third article describes the conceptual basis for carrying capacity determination. It was the basis for a later book on carrying capacity (annotated below). The fourth article reviews the evolution of the carrying capacity concept. The authors suggest that research should focus on the question of what kinds of resource and social conditions are appropriate and acceptable in different settings. This concept—the Limits of Acceptable Change—became the basis for the LAC planning process, which has become the most widely used wilderness-management planning framework. The fifth article calls for managers to draw a clear distinction between facts and judgments in decisionmaking, and advocates for "biosocial systems analysis" as a clear and more equitable method for allocating resources. The sixth article levels some severe criticisms against past approaches to understanding carrying capacity. The author emphasizes that science can aid managers in making resource allocation decisions, but it cannot be the sole basis for them. The seventh and final article summarizes what is known and what remains to be determined about social carrying capacity.

Shelby, Bo; Heberlein, Thomas A. 1986. Carrying capacity in recreation settings. Corvallis, OR: Oregon State University Press. 164 p.

Annotation: This book develops a model for carrying capacity research and management based on a literature review and indepth case studies from six locations. The authors suggest that readers study the first chapter, which describes the carrying capacity model, then decide which of the remaining six chapters to pursue. Chapter 2 describes the case studies that the authors make reference to in the rest of the book. Chapters 3 through 5 consider different approaches for developing evaluative capacity standards. These chapters focus on visitor satisfaction, perceived crowding, and encounter preferences, respectively. Chapter 6 describes how to apply the carrying capacity model in different settings, including a wilderness backpacking area. The authors describe the Carrying Capacity Assessment Process (C-CAP), which is a step-by-step process for determining capacities, similar to the Limits of Acceptable Change (LAC) and Visitor Impact Management (VIM) processes. In addition, they detail steps for conducting carrying capacity studies, discuss approaches to incorporating capacity research into policy and management decisions, and present important considerations and methods for allocating resources. In three appendices, the authors present technical information for setting up and conducting carrying

capacity studies and for setting up permit systems to allocate and evaluate use.

2. Limits of Acceptable Change (LAC)

McCool, Stephen F.; Cole, David N., comps. 1997. Proceedings—Limits of Acceptable Change and related planning processes: progress and future directions; 1997 May 20–22; Missoula, MT. Gen. Tech. Rep. INT-371. Ogden, UT: U.S. Department of Agriculture, Forest Service, Rocky Mountain Research Station. 84 p.

Annotation: This workshop proceedings contains eight invited papers, three synthesis papers, and a short annotated bibliography. The purpose of the workshop was to evaluate and learn from experience in applying Limits of Acceptable Change (LAC) processes. LAC processes have different titles but share major features. They include Visitor Impact Management (VIM) and Visitor Experience and Resource Protection (VERP), as well as Limits of Acceptable Change (LAC). Invited papers comprise the bulk of this publication. Among other items, the authors of these papers discuss the original intent of LAC, evaluate their experiences with applying LAC, and compare differences between LAC processes. The synthesis papers discuss suggested modifications of LAC processes, extensions of LAC beyond recreation in protected areas, and lessons learned from 15 years of applying LAC. The annotated bibliography contains references that may be useful for someone interested in using an LAC process—most of which are included in this reading list.

Stankey, George H.; Cole, David N.; Lucas, Robert C.; Petersen, Margaret E.; Frissell, Sidney S. 1985. The Limits of Acceptable Change (LAC) system for wilderness planning. Gen. Tech. Rep. INT-176. Ogden, UT: U.S. Department of Agriculture, Forest Service, Intermountain Forest and Range Experiment Station. 37 p.

Annotation: This document describes the LAC system for establishing appropriate resource and social conditions in recreation settings. LAC differs from carrying capacity in that the focus is on desirable conditions rather than how much use an area can tolerate. The LAC process involves nine steps: (1) identification of area concerns; (2) description of opportunity classes; (3) identification of indicators; (4) inventory of existing conditions; (5) definition of standards for each indicator; (6) identification of alternative area allocations; (7) analysis of costs and benefits of alternatives; (8) selection of a final alternative; and (9) implementation of selected alternative and establishment of a monitoring program. Following a description of each of these steps, a hypothetical example of implementing the LAC process in a wilderness area is provided.

3. Visitor Impact Management (VIM)

Graefe, Alan R.; Kuss, Fred R.; Vaske, Jerry J. 1990. Visitor impact management: the planning framework: volume 2. Washington DC: National Parks and Conservation Association. 105 p.

Annotation: This volume and volume 1 (see below) are designed to be used together to provide a comprehensive synthesis of empirical and theoretical work related to carrying capacity, and to provide a framework for visitor impact management in various National Park settings. In volume 1, the authors briefly describe the difference between carrying capacity, which is focused on visitor use levels, and the broader concept of visitor impact management, which recognizes that manipulating use levels is but one way of reducing recreation impacts. The remainder of the volume is dedicated to a review and synthesis of past work. Chapters are divided according to impacts on vegetation and soils, water resources, wildlife, and visitor experiences. In the concluding chapter, the authors identify five issues that should be included within any visitor impact management program: impact interrelationships, use-impact relationships, varying tolerance to impacts, activity-specific influences, and site-specific influences. Volume 2 describes the Visitor Impact Management (VIM) planning framework. The authors begin by reviewing the five issues identified in volume 1. In following chapters, they present eight principles for visitor impact management, eight steps for assessing and managing visitor impacts, and six case studies of VIM implementation. Five appendices at the end of the document ar: (A) checklist of questions for identification of impact problems and potential solutions; (B) sample impact assessment tools; (C) sample systems for classification of areas by level of impact; (D) review of existing management and planning frameworks; and (E) summary of scientific research considerations.

Kuss, Fred R.; Graefe, Alan R.; Vaske, Jerry J. 1990. Visitor impact management: a review of research: volume 1. Washington, DC: National Parks and Conservation Association: 187–217.

Annotation: This report is volume 1 of a two-volume set. The annotation for both volumes is given under Graefe and others (1990) above.

4. Visitor Experience and Resource Protection (VERP)

Hof, Marilyn; Lime, David W. 1997. Visitor experience and resource protection framework in the National Park system: rational, current status, and future direction. Proceedings—Limits of Acceptable Change and related planning processes: progress and future directions; 1997 May 20–22; Missoula, MT. Gen. Tech. Rep. INT-371. Ogden, UT: U.S. Department of Agriculture, Forest Service, Rocky Mountain Research Station: 29–36.

Annotation: In response to the perception that the National Park Service was failing to systematically address visitor use and impacts, an interdisciplinary team of Park Service personnel and researchers began developing the Visitor Experience and Resource Protection (VERP) planning framework in the early 1990s. This paper compares VERP to other planning frameworks, assesses past experience in applying VERP, and considers changes that may be needed in the future. Conceptually, VERP does not differ from LAC or other related planning processes. The primary difference in VERP is that it is driven by goals defined by park purpose, while LAC tends to be more issue driven. VERP is also designed to address frontcountry issues common in many National Parks. The

authors suggest that VERP has been a success so far, although they caution that it remains relatively new and has only been applied at a few places so far. The future changes they suggest are related to creating institutional settings in which all levels of management are committed, financially and otherwise, to full implementation of the VERP framework.

U.S. Department of the Interior, National Park Service. 1997. The Visitor Experience and Resource Protection (VERP) framework: a handbook for planners and managers. Denver, CO: Denver Service Center. 103 p.

Annotation: This handbook is primarily intended for National Park Service planners and managers to use as a general guide for the application of VERP planning in units of the National Park System. However, it may be useful for personnel from other agencies and organizations as well. The first portion of the handbook gives an overview of the carrying capacity concept and the VERP framework. The next section, which comprises the bulk of the document, describes the nine VERP framework elements: (1) assemble an interdisciplinary project team; (2) develop a public involvement strategy; (3) develop statements of park purpose; identify planning constraints; (4) analyze park resources an existing use; (5) describe a potential range of visitor experiences and resource conditions; (6) allocate potential zones; (7) select indicators and standards for each zone; develop a monitoring plan; (8) monitor indicators; and (9) take management action. The final portion of the handbook provides examples of the first application of VERP at Arches National Park. A glossary of terms and a bibliography of useful references are also provided.

C. Identifying Indicators and Setting Standards

Indicators are defined broadly here as elements of wilderness settings or visitor experiences that may change in response to human activities. Standards are defined as predetermined levels of indicators that guide management actions. Selecting indicators and standards of wilderness experience quality has proven to be a challenging task for researchers and managers alike. With regard to indicators, the primary challenge has been identifying the most important ones from the myriad possibilities. Setting standards is made difficult because there are no absolute criteria for determining appropriate indicator levels. The authors in this section describe ways to measure, evaluate, and select indicators, and present several different approaches to determining and prescribing appropriate standards.

Cole, David N. 1994. The wilderness threats matrix: a framework for assessing impacts. Res. Pap. INT-475. Ogden, UT: U.S. Department of Agriculture, Forest Service, Intermountain Research Station. 14 p.

Annotation: This research paper describes the development and application of a framework for assessing wilderness threats. The framework is depicted as a matrix with potential threats to wilderness as columns and wilderness attributes as rows. Cells in the matrix represent the impacts of each threat on each attribute. Threats are defined as human activities or consequences of human activities that have potential to change wilderness conditions. Although interactive or cumulative effects of some threats may be important, they are not depicted in the matrix. A wilderness research team identified the eight most significant threats to wilderness attributes in the Forest Service Northern Region: (1) recreation, (2) livestock, (3) mining, (4) fire, (5) exotic species, (6) water projects, (7) atmospheric pollutants, and (8) adjacent lands. An "other" category was also included as a threat column in the matrix. General attributes that apply in all wilderness areas were identified as air, aquatic systems, landforms, soils, vegetation, animals, ecosystems/landscapes, cultural resources, and wilderness experiences. Although this matrix was specifically designed for Forest Service wilderness in Montana and Idaho, similar matrices could be developed for other regions. The threats matrix may help managers think more comprehensively about monitoring in wilderness, and it can be used by planners at all stages of planning.

Hollenhorst, Steven; Gardner, Lisa. 1994. The indicator performance estimate approach to determining acceptable wilderness conditions. Environmental Management. 18(6): 901–906.

Annotation: With regard to choosing indicators of experience quality for wilderness management planning, two major limitations have arisen: (1) lack of knowledge about the importance of indicators relative to quality wilderness experiences; and (2) difficulties in comparing conditions or performance of indicators. Indicator performance is defined as the difference between visitor standards and actual conditions. This paper describes the use of an importance-performance approach to prioritize wilderness indicators. A procedure for calculating Indicator Performance Estimates (IPEs) and locating them within a four-quadrant matrix is described. Labels describe the suggested management strategy for addressing items that fall within each quadrant. For instance, indicators with high indicator performance scores and high importance scores fall into the upper right quadrant of the matrix labeled "keep up the good work." Indicators with low IPEs and high importance scores fall into the upper left quadrant of the matrix labeled "concentrate here." The authors applied their IPE approach in a study conducted during summer 1991 at the Cranberry Wilderness Area in West Virginia. They identified, among other items, four indicators related to feelings of crowding that fell into the "concentrate here" category. A significant advantage of the IPE approach is that managers may directly compare the importance of indicators relative to visitor standards.

Merigliano, Linda L. 1989. Indicators to monitor the wilderness recreation experience. In: Lime, David W., ed. Managing America's enduring wilderness resource; 1989 September 11–17; Minneapolis, MN. St. Paul: University of Minnesota Extension Service: 156–162.

Annotation: In this paper, indicators are defined as specific elements of the wilderness setting that change in response to human activities. The author lists and discusses nine descriptive criteria for selecting indicators, including: quantitative, correlation, feasible, reliable, responsive, sensitive, integration, early warning, and significance. Good indicators to monitor the wilderness experience reflect the ability of an area to provide visitors with the opportunity to receive beneficial physical and psychological outcomes. Six categories of benefits of

wilderness experience have been identified in past studies: solitude, closeness to nature, freedom of choice, challenge, intragroup intimacy, and health. In the final portion of this paper, potential indicators that reflect the ability of an area to provide opportunities for each of these benefits are listed.

Roggenbuck, J. W.; Williams, D. R.; Watson, A. E. 1993. Defining acceptable conditions in wilderness. Environmental Management. 17(2): 187–197.

Annotation: This article describes an effort to compare visitor perceptions of appropriate conditions across four different wilderness areas. See complete annotation in section III.A.1, page 15.

Shelby, Bo; Shindler, Bruce. 1992. Interest group standards for ecological impacts at wilderness campsites. Leisure Sciences. 14: 17–27.

Annotation: See section III.A.1, page 16.

Shelby, Bo; Stankey, George; Shindler, Bruce, tech. eds. 1992. Defining wilderness quality: the role of standards in wilderness management—a workshop proceedings; 1990 April 10-11; Fort Collins, CO. Gen. Tech. Rep. PNW-305. Portland, OR: U.S. Department of Agriculture, Forest Service, Pacific Northwest Research Station. 114 p.

Annotation: This document contains 14 papers that were developed from a 1990 workshop to discuss the role of standards in wilderness management. The first six papers are listed under the section heading "Research." These papers address criteria for selecting standards, provide examples and discussion of the normative approach to standard selection, and discuss standards for nonwilderness areas and nonrecreational values. Next are two papers that make cases for and against uniform national standards for wilderness. The five remaining papers cover specific examples and case studies of the use of standards for wilderness management by the Forest Service, Bureau of Land Management, and the National Park Service.

Shelby, Bo; Vaske, Jerry J.; Harris, Rick. 1988. User standards for ecological impacts at wilderness campsites. Journal of Leisure Research. 20(3): 245–256.

Annotation: See section III.A.1, page 16.

Tarrant, Michael A.; Shafer, C. Scott. 1997. Condition indicators for distinct wilderness: is there uniformity? International Journal of Wilderness. 3(4): 29–33.

Annotation: The argument for uniform national wilderness standards recognizes that all wilderness areas are part of a nationwide system and therefore should be maintained to minimum standards in order to provide similar quality recreation experiences. The argument against uniformity is that conditions across wilderness areas are so diverse that standards would not be comparable. To address this issue, this paper explores the extent to which visitor concerns and perceptions of conditions are similar across three distinct wilderness areas: Cohutta in Tennessee and Georgia, Comanche Peak in Colorado, and Okeefenokee in southern Georgia. Litter, vegetation damage, and noise were among the top concerns in all three user groups. However, visitors to the Eastern wilderness areas were significantly less concerned with amount of noise heard from outside the wilderness, and number of groups that pass within sight of camp, than Comanche Peak visitors. Overall, there were significant differences between the user groups in level of concern for wilderness conditions and in perceptions of existing conditions within the respective wilderness areas. The authors suggest that there may be support for a limited number of uniform standards, including litter, vegetation damage, and opportunities to view wildlife. Other conditions varied by area in terms of their importance and influence on visitors. Therefore, the question of uniformity versus variety in standards may depend on the type of condition being considered.

Watson, Alan; Cole, David. 1992. LAC indicators: an evaluation of progress and list of proposed indicators. In: Merigliano, Linda, ed. Ideas for Limits of Acceptable Change process: book two. Washington, DC: U.S. Department of Agriculture, Forest Service, Recreation Staff: 65–84.

Annotation: This paper compares desirable characteristics of indicators with a list of indicators that have been proposed or adopted in management plans in order to evaluate progress and problems related to selecting Limits of Acceptable Change indicators. Based on an evaluation of 24 different LAC plans, the authors provide a list of general conditions or areas of concern—termed factors—and their corresponding indicators. Three types of problems related to selecting indicators are identified: (1) difficulty in defining indicators in specific quantitative terms; (2) difficulty in selecting among indicators because of lack of understanding about which are most significant; and (3) lack of reliable monitoring methods.

Watson, Alan E.; Roggenbuck, Joseph W. 1996. Selecting human experience indicators for wilderness: different approaches provide different results. In: Kulhavy, David L.; Legg, Michael H., eds. Wilderness and natural areas in Eastern North America: research, management and planning. Nacogdoches, TX: Stephen F. Austin State University, Arthur Temple College of Forestry, Center for Applied Studies: 264–269.

Annotation: This book chapter focuses on alternative methods for selecting and determining the significance of wilderness experience indicators. Three primary ways that decisions about indicator significance have traditionally been made are working groups, public response to agency proposals, and visitor surveys. The bulk of this chapter addresses methods aimed at improving the third approach—visitor surveys. Most surveys include a pool of indicators developed in advance by researchers. This approach may strongly influence the set of items determined to be significant. At the Juniper Prairie Wilderness in Florida, two alternative approaches were used to understand the dimensions of visitor experiences so that a list of specific local indicators could be developed. In the first approach, visitors were asked to record their focus of attention and feelings about various items at multiple, randomly selected points during their experiences. In the second study, open-ended interviews were conducted with groups of visitors immediately following their trips. Both studies provided new insight into the nature of visitor experiences and were useful in identifying meaningful indicators for management planning.

Williams, Daniel R.; Roggenbuck, Joseph W.; Patterson, Michael E.; Watson, Alan E. 1992b. The variability of user-based social impact standards for wilderness management. Forest Science. 38(4): 738–756.

Annotation: The social norm concept has been widely used to develop standards for social impact indicators in outdoor recreation settings. An issue of increasing concern is the variability within impact norm judgments. The purpose of this paper is to identify the magnitude of four sources of variance (subject, occasion, area, and indicator) and to make recommendations regarding the number and types of indicators to monitor, the number of respondents necessary to achieve reliable estimates of impact standards, and the applicability of social impact standards across wilderness areas. Using a model known as Generalizability Theory to analyze data from surveys conducted at three Eastern and one Western wilderness area, the authors found: (1) subject variability (differences between respondents) may be controlled by obtaining a large sample; (2) variance due to occasion (time and place of survey) was modest, suggesting that standards are generalizable from one occasion to another; and (3) social condition standards are generalizable across areas. Finally, the authors report that high subject variability puts into question the degree to which normative standards exist. They suggest future research to further investigate the nature of between-subject variability.

D. Monitoring Visitor Experiences

Monitoring visitor experiences is a fundamental component of wilderness management planning. The authors in this section describe specific reasons for monitoring social conditions (Watson 1990), and present strategies for monitoring at the local wilderness level (Martin 1989; Watson and others 1998) as well as at the National Wilderness System level (Landres and others 1994). In addition, Ashor (2000) presents results from 10 years of monitoring at a small Montana wilderness area.

Ashor, Joe L. 2000. Monitoring social indicators in the Bear Trap Canyon Wilderness 1988–1998. In: Cole, David N.; McCool, Stephen F.; Borrie, William T.; O'Loughlin, Jennifer, comps. Wilderness science in a time of change conference—volume 4: wilderness visitors, experiences, and visitor management; 1999 May 23–27; Missoula, MT. Proc. RMRS-P-0-VOL-4. Ogden, UT: U.S. Department of Agriculture, Forest Service, Rocky Mountain Research Station: 229–231.

Annotation: This paper presents a case study of monitoring over 10-years in a small wilderness in Montana. Analysis of monitoring data shows that there is only a weak relationship between use levels and the ability to meet Limits of Acceptable Change (LAC) social standards. That is, increases in numbers of users do not necessarily increase the likelihood of encountering other users in the wilderness. Similarly, decreases in use do not necessarily reduce the likelihood of encounters. The author suggests that visitors adjust the timing of their trips to weekdays and evening hours to avoid crowding when use levels increase. Although many factors other than management action may influence social conditions in the wilderness, the author emphasizes that managers need to act consistently to maintain the condition of indicators within determined standards.

Landres, Peter; Cole, David; Watson, Alan. 1994. A monitoring strategy for the National Wilderness Preservation System. In: Hendee, John C.; Martin, Vance G., eds. International wilderness allocation, management, and research. Fort

Collins, CO: International Wilderness Leadership (WILD) Foundation: 192–197.

Annotation: The diversity of the National Wilderness Preservation System (NWPS) renders any single monitoring program developed for one area inadequate to meet issues of concern for the whole system. The authors of this paper propose a comprehensive monitoring strategy as an umbrella under which individual units of the NWPS can develop specific programs to fit their needs. Three primary purposes for all wilderness monitoring are to improve wilderness management, to improve the acquisition and use of knowledge from wilderness, and to improve assessment of the status and trends of the NWPS. These purposes form the basis of a conceptual model for a national monitoring strategy. Each broad purpose suggests several subcategories of information that needs to be collected and monitored. The authors propose a method for implementing a national monitoring program whereby managers develop initial recommendations, scientists summarize existing knowledge and identify gaps, and each group revises their input in an iterative process. Each iteration provides the opportunity to review successes and failures and incorporate the newest information.

Martin, Steven R. 1989. A framework for monitoring experiential conditions in wilderness. In: Lime, David W., ed. Managing America's enduring wilderness resource; 1989 September 11–17; Minneapolis, MN. St. Paul: University of Minnesota Extension Service: 170–175.

Annotation: This paper outlines a seven-step process to help managers develop an experiential monitoring program: (1) understand the rationale for monitoring; (2) review what has been done by others; (3) decide what to monitor; (4) determine how to monitor; (5) know what to do with the data before they are collected (6) implement monitoring; and (7) use the information. Each step is explained in detail and a summary list emphasizing important points is presented at the end of the paper.

Merigliano, Linda L. 1989. Indicators to monitor wilderness conditions. In: Lime, David W., ed. Managing America's enduring wilderness resource; 1989 September 11–17; Minneapolis, MN. St. Paul: University of Minnesota Extension Service: 205–209.

Annotation: See section IV.C, page 26.

Watson, Alan E. 1990. Why is it important to monitor social conditions in wilderness? In: Lime, David W., ed. Managing America's enduring wilderness resource; 1989 September 11–17; Minneapolis, MN. St. Paul: University of Minnesota Extension Service: 150–155.

Annotation: This paper discusses reasons for monitoring use levels, use trends, and the quality of recreation experiences. General reasons for monitoring use levels and use trends include: (1) increase accuracy of legislatively mandated demand projections and meet National Forest Management Act regulations; (2) facilitate specification of feasible objectives and selection of management objectives to achieve them; and (3) give more credibility to requests for funding of management programs. The goal of providing quality recreation experiences is widely accepted by wilderness managers and researchers. Specific reasons for monitoring the quality of experiences include the requirements of various national legislation such as the Wilderness Act, National Forest Management Act,

Resource Planning Act, and National Environmental Policy Act. In addition, most planning systems—such as Limits of Acceptable Change—require monitoring of social conditions.

Watson, Alan E.; Cronn, Rich; Christensen, Neal A. 1998. Monitoring inter-group encounters in wilderness. Res. Pap. RMRS-RP-14. Fort Collins, CO: U.S. Department of Agriculture, Forest Service, Rocky Mountain Research Station. 20 p.

Annotation: Although measures of intergroup visitor encounters are popular indicators in many LAC-type management plans, monitoring these indicators can be challenging. The purpose of this paper is to improve understanding of encounter monitoring methods. The authors describe a study conducted to accomplish three objectives: (1) provide estimates of encounter rates by various methods; (2) determine the relationship between the various measures of encounter rates; and (3) determine the relationship between various indirect predictors of encounter rates and actual encounter rates. Six systems were used to measure encounter rates at the Alpine Lakes Wilderness in Washington in 1991. These systems included exit surveys, trip diaries, trained observers, wilderness ranger observations, mechanical counters, trailhead counts, and parking lot vehicle counts. Estimates of encounter rates varied substantially across methods used. On high-use trails, visitor perceptions of group encounter frequencies were lower than those of trained observers. On lightly used trails, visitor reports were higher than those of trained observers. The authors emphasize that differences in estimates cannot necessarily be used to determine which method is best, because different methods may measure slightly different things. For instance, exit surveys and trip diaries measure encounters as perceived by the visitor. Observer methods measure encounters witnessed by the trained observer. Good indicators must be specific enough to guide selection of the appropriate method. Results from this study can help managers decide which method is most appropriate for a given area. In addition, they may also encourage more precise definition of indicators.

Watson, Alan E; Cole, David N.; Turner, David L; Reynolds, Penny S. 2000. Wilderness recreation use estimation: a handbook of methods and systems. Gen. Tech. Rep. RMRS-GTR-56. Ogden, UT: U.S. Department of Agriculture, Forest Service, Rocky Mountain Research Station. 198 p.

Annotation: Although there is a clear need for accurate information about the amount, types, and distribution of wilderness recreation use, research shows that most wilderness managers do not employ reliable, systematic procedures for gathering this information. This report is designed to be a comprehensive source that managers can use to guide themselves through the process of designing and conducting use estimation plans. The authors describe use estimation as a conceptual system that includes five component parts: setting objectives, identifying which use characteristics to measure, developing a sampling plan, collecting data, and calculating and reporting basic statistics. The report is divided into three main sections. The first section describes the basic steps for choosing and implementing a use-estimation system. The second section describes 10 different use-estimation systems in detail. The final section contains formulas and procedures for calculating and reporting basic statistics.

AUTHOR INDEX

Rocky Mountain Research Station
240 West Prospect Road
Fort Collins, CO 80526

RMRS
ROCKY MOUNTAIN RESEARCH STATION

The Rocky Mountain Research Station develops scientific information and technology to improve management, protection, and use of the forests and rangelands. Research is designed to meet the needs of National Forest managers, Federal and State agencies, public and private organizations, academic institutions, industry, and individuals.

Studies accelerate solutions to problems involving ecosystems, range, forests, water, recreation, fire, resource inventory, land reclamation, community sustainability, forest engineering technology, multiple use economics, wildlife and fish habitat, and forest insects and diseases. Studies are conducted cooperatively, and applications may be found worldwide.

Research Locations

Flagstaff, Arizona	Reno, Nevada
Fort Collins, Colorado*	Albuquerque, New Mexico
Boise, Idaho	Rapid City, South Dakota
Moscow, Idaho	Logan, Utah
Bozeman, Montana	Ogden, Utah
Missoula, Montana	Provo, Utah
Lincoln, Nebraska	Laramie, Wyoming

*Station Headquarters, Natural Resources Research Center, 2150 Centre Avenue, Building A, Fort Collins, CO 80526